91 COOL MATH TRICKS

to Make you Gasp!

ANNA CLAYBOURNE

ARCTURUS

This edition published in 2021 by Arcturus Publishing Limited
26/27 Bickels Yard, 151–153 Bermondsey Street,
London SE1 3HA

Author: Anna Claybourne
Illustrator: Josephine Wolff
Editors: Stephanie Carey and Cloud King Creative
Designer: Nathan Balsom
Design Manager: Jessica Holliland
Editorial Manager: Joe Harris

ISBN: 978-1-83940-617-1
CH007354NT
Supplier 29, Date 0921, Print run 11958

Printed in China

What is STEM?

STEM is a world-wide initiative that aims to cultivate an interest in Science, Technology, Engineering, and Mathematics, in an effort to promote these disciplines to as wide a variety of students as possible.

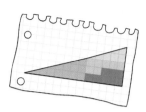

CONTENTS

INTRODUCTION

If you want to discover all kinds of mindbending mathematics tricks, games, challenges, and mysteries, this is the book for you. You won't believe the amazing things that mathematics can do!

What is mathematics?

You know what mathematics is when you do it at school—but what does it really mean?

Mathematics is the science of numbers, measuring, and calculating. It's not just a school subject—it's used in all kinds of science, and it's pretty important in everyday life, too. Here are some daily tasks for which mathematics is important:

Our money systems, which allow people to buy things, save, or get paid . . .

Marking dates and times, so that we know when we're doing stuff . . .

Measuring things, so that we can build houses that aren't wobbly, or mix the correct ingredients to make a cake . . .

Figuring out angles and directions, so that we can do things like making sure a spacecraft gets to the moon . . .

Adding labels to things, so we can find the right address, bus, or shoe size.

Mathematics makes sense to everyone around the world, because numbers work in the same basic way everywhere.

But the more you look into the world of numbers, the more mysterious and magical things you find. How can you cut a strip of paper in two so that there's still only one piece? How do you make a square appear from nowhere? What's the secret to drawing a perfect star every time? How can you make an impossible piece of paper, create an (almost!) uncrackable code, or fool your friends into thinking that you can read their minds?

…and just what DID Archimedes discover in the bath?

This book is stuffed with cool tricks and mathematical magic, designed to blow your mind. Try to solve the puzzles yourself first— then use them to baffle your friends and family!

THE MYSTERIOUS MISSING SQUARE

For our first trick, we'll make a square appear and disappear—from nowhere!
Once you've figured out how it works, try it on your unsuspecting friends and family.

the trick

First, look at this triangle jigsaw, made up of four smaller shapes. It's on a squared background, so you can see exactly how many squares long and high each piece is.

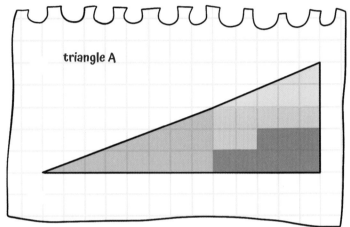

triangle A

Perfectly normal triangle—nothing to see here!

Got it? Now look at the triangle below. It's made of the EXACT SAME SHAPES, rearranged. The height and length of the triangle are the same. All the pieces are the same, too. And yet ... this triangle has a square that's not filled in! How did that happen?

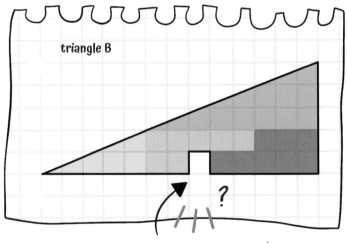

triangle B

?

Hang on ...there's a spare square!

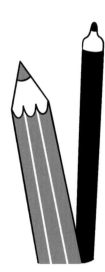

What's going on?

So how does it work? Well, actually, we lied. These are NOT normal triangles—in fact, they are not triangles at all. If you hold a ruler next to the long, sloping edge of each triangle, you'll find it's not a straight line. In triangle A, it dips down slightly where piece 1 meets piece 2. But when the pieces are rearranged to make triangle B, the line sticks up slightly.

The difference is very slight, so both triangles look normal at first glance. However, because of the difference between them, triangle B is one square bigger that triangle A.

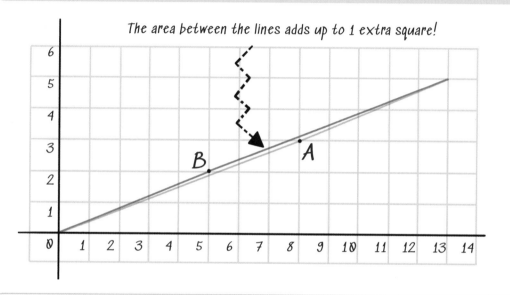

The area between the lines adds up to 1 extra square!

Did you know?

To fool your friends, you can actually draw the shapes on graph paper, and cut them out, then arrange them on another piece of graph paper.

When you rearrange them, the extra square appears!

HOW MANY SQUARES?

This trick is pretty simple. All you have to do is count the squares! How hard can it be?

The trick

Look at this picture, and count how many squares you can see. Take as long as you like. You could ask a friend or family member to try it, too. Write down your answers, then compare them.

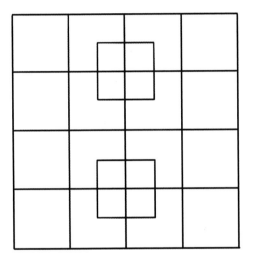

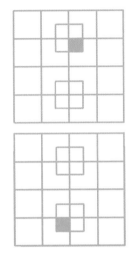

How did you do? Did you get 40 squares? If not, don't worry—most people don't. (But if you did spot 40 squares, well done—you are a mathematical genius!)

The small squares are easy to spot . . .

But you have to count the medium-sized squares, too.

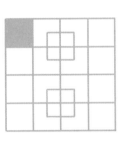

What's going on?

Puzzles like this can easily fool you, because you might not notice that the lines in the picture make up bigger, hidden squares as well as smaller ones.

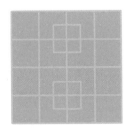

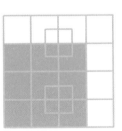

Don't forget the big one around the outside!

HOW MANY TRIANGLES?

Now you know what to do, trying this triangle teaser should be a breeze.

The trick

Here's your picture. How many triangles can you count?
It looks simple, but take care—it's tougher than it looks!

If you're stuck, try starting with the smallest size of triangle.
Count them, then look for the next size up, and the next size up,
and so on. With this method, if you do it carefully,
you should find 24 triangles in total!

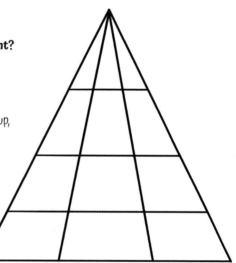

What's going on?

Some people find this puzzle even harder than the squares one! It's not only hard to spot all the triangles, it's also tricky to keep track of which ones you've already counted.

If you want to be really sure (and have all day!), try drawing the shape out lots of times, and shading in each triangle separately.

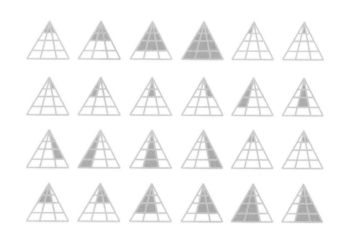

Try these versions, too!

SHAPE STRETCHER

This trick uses mathematical principles to make a clever stretched drawing. When you look at it from the right angle, you see a perfect picture! It's where mathematics meets art.

The trick

These pictures are called "anamorphic" drawings. Artists use them to make hidden images and 3D trick pictures. Here's an example . . .

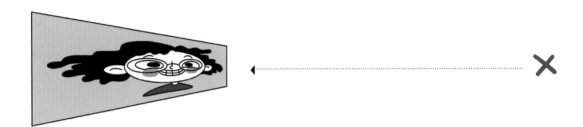

This picture looks stretched and distorted. But put one eye close to the X mark on the page, and look at it again. The picture looks normal! Try the trick yourself—you'll need two grids, like the ones below: a stretched one and a normal one. You can copy or trace these grids, or draw your own.

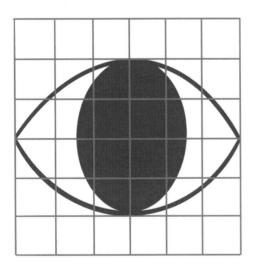

On the square grid, draw your picture normally. Then copy your picture onto the stretched grid. Copy one square at a time, stretching the lines and shapes to fit, like this:

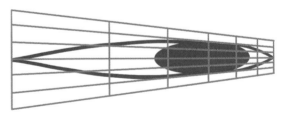

Finally, trace your stretched picture onto plain paper. Shade it in, if you like. When you look at it from one end, you'll see the picture normally!

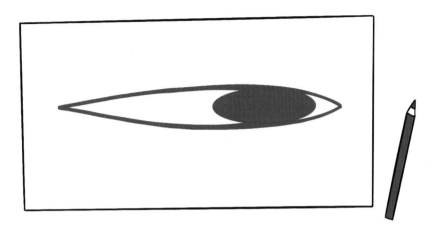

What's going on?

As you know, things that are farther away look smaller. If you draw a picture that gets bigger and more stretched out at one end, this makes up for the "shrinking" effect. So when you look at it from the right angle, the stretched parts look smaller, and it looks normal.

Now try this!

If you draw a ball this way on a piece of paper, then look at it from the end, it will look like a 3D ball that's floating! Cut out the top half of the ball and add a shadow underneath to make it even more convincing.

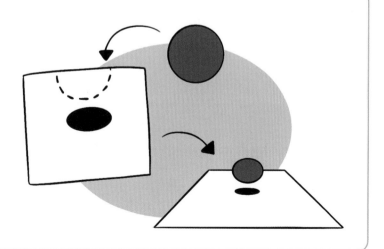

DRAW A STAR, ANY STAR!

Would you like to be able to draw perfect stars, with any number of points?
Well, now's your chance! Just try this easy trick—the secret mathematical star formula.

the trick

First, draw a circle using a compass, or by tracing around a circular object. For a simple five-pointed star, draw five dots around the edge of the circle, spaced out evenly.

Now start at one dot, and draw a line to the next-but-one dot around the circle, as shown below. Keep going using the same pattern, drawing a line to the next-but-one dot, until you get back to where you started.

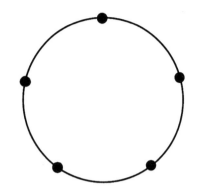

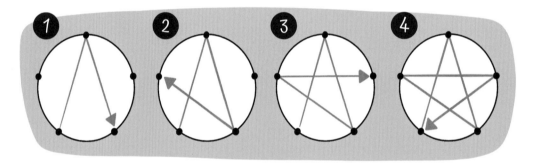

Finally, erase the circle and any lines you don't want, or trace your finished star.

Ta-da, a star!

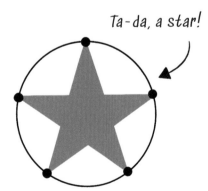

That was easy! But it gets better—you can use the same method to draw other star types, too. First, draw any number of dots around the circle. Then draw a line from one dot to the next-but-one dot, and keep going.

Or, for a pointier star, you can skip two dots each time, or three dots.

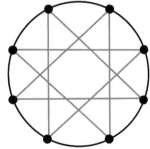

If you get back to where you started, and the star isn't finished, just start again from a different dot, like this:

 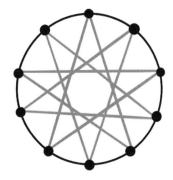

What's going on?

Stars are a type of polygon—a mathematical shape with straight sides.
If you always count the same number of dots around the circle when drawing your lines,
the points of the star will always have the same angle as each other, and it will look perfect.

Use your stars in drawings and decorations, or to make mobiles.

DON'T COVER YOUR tRACKS!

This trick is known as a Euler puzzle, after Swiss genius, Leonhard Euler. He spent years pondering puzzles like these in the 1700s.

the trick

Here's a simple Euler puzzle to start with, known as a Euler house. Your challenge is to draw this shape on a piece of paper. Easy, right? But wait! You must draw it as one continuous line, without lifting your pencil from the paper, and you can't trace the same line twice. (Crossing lines is allowed!)

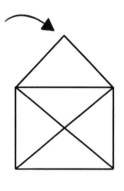

Did you manage it? It can be done. As long as you start from a bottom corner, and end at the other one, there are several ways to do it. Here's one:

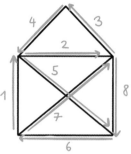

OK, now try this one . . . It's a bit harder, isn't it? In fact, it's impossible!

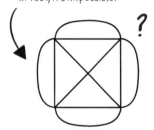

Here are a few more to try. Can you tell by looking at them which ones are possible?

What's going on?

You can't go over the same line twice. So whenever you arrive at a junction, you must leave along a different line. That means that all the junctions you go through must have an even number of lines joining them. Only the start and end points can have an odd number of lines. Simple!

Here's a similar trick, but this one's a bit sneakier. Try it on a friend or family member!

The trick

Challenge them to draw a circle with a dot in the middle without lifting their pen from the paper.

When they're stumped, show them how! First, draw the dot,
then fold the edge of the paper over so that the edge touches the dot.

Draw on the back of the paper until you're a little distance away from the dot,
then unfold the paper and draw your circle!

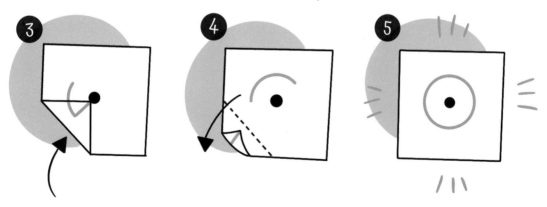

What's going on?

It may seem impossible—until you remember that a piece of paper has two sides!
(Well, except for the piece of paper on page 50, but that's another story . . .)

THE CURIOUS CAFE WALL

This bizarre trick will turn straight strips of paper into wobbly ones, before your very eyes!

The trick

First, you need to make a chessboard pattern.

Take a piece of white paper, then use a ruler and pencil to draw lines across it, roughly every 2.5 cm (1 inch). Do the same up and down the paper, to make a grid.

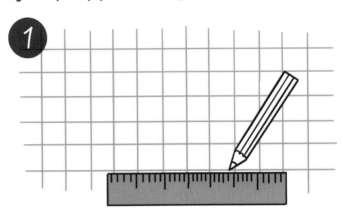

Now shade in every other square with a black pen or marker, like this, to make a chessboard pattern.

Next, cut along the horizontal lines to make chessboard strips, like these . . .

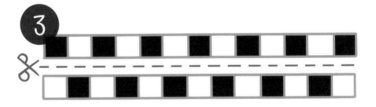

Last, put your strips on top of another piece of paper that's a different shade. Arrange them so that the black squares make wavy lines, like this . . .

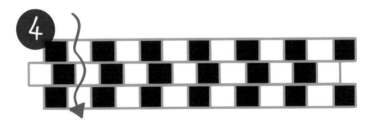

...and this is what it will look like!

When you get them in the right position, they'll suddenly look tilted and wobbly—even though you know they're not.

What's going on?

This trick works because of the way your brain senses straight and diagonal lines.
The leaning towers of tiles make them appear to tilt where they overlap with the white tiles.
As this happens all the way along, your brain sees the lines in between as diagonal.

Making actual chessboard strips lets you experiment with the illusion,
and prove to your friends that the lines really are straight!

Did you know?

This illusion is known as the "cafe wall illusion." It got that name because it was first spotted on an actual cafe wall, which was covered in tiles in this pattern.

SQUARE THE CIRCLES

When you perform this sneaky trick, everyone will be amazed that you can actually turn two circles into one square! You'll need two strips of paper, tape, scissors—and magical mathematical know-how.

The trick

First, make two loops of paper. Cut two strips of paper about 2.5 cm (1 inch) wide, and 20 cm (8 inches) long. Tape the ends together on both sides to make the loops.

These are your two circles. Show them to your audience, and tell them you can make them into a square. Can they guess how? Bet they can't!

Here's how to do it ... Put the two loops together at right angles to each other, and tape them together on both sides of the join.

Now take your scissors, and start cutting along the middle of one of the loops. Cut all the way around it until you cut it in two. Now you'll have this:

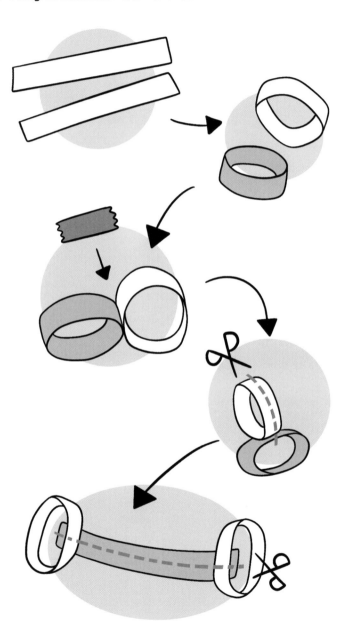

Finally, cut along the middle of the other strip too. And there's your square!

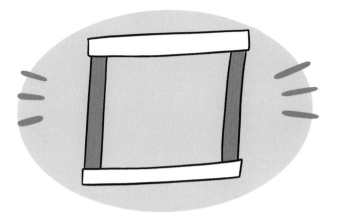

What's going on?

Your two circles didn't look like a square, but once you taped them together, they were. The right-angled join made four square corners—they were just stuck together. The strips made straight sides—but they were curled into circles. By cutting along the strips, you separated the corners and sides from each other, and a square was born!

THROUGH THE POSTCARD

For this next trick, show your audience a totally normal postcard, and tell them you can walk right through it. (Just make sure it's not a postcard that anyone wants to keep!)

the trick

Pretty soon, everyone will be asking to see exactly HOW you walk through a postcard.

So here's how to do it. (You may want to try it out on your own, first!)

Fold your postcard in half lengthways, with the picture on the inside.

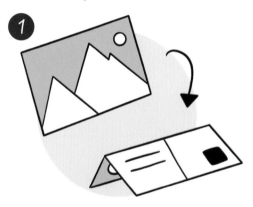

1

Take a pen, and draw lines on the folded postcard. Copy the picture carefully!

2

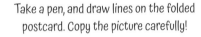

Now use scissors to cut very carefully along all the lines. Make sure you don't cut beyond the end of each line.

3

Cut from here ...

Unfold the postcard, then cut along the fold you made. Start at one of the cuts nearest one end.

4

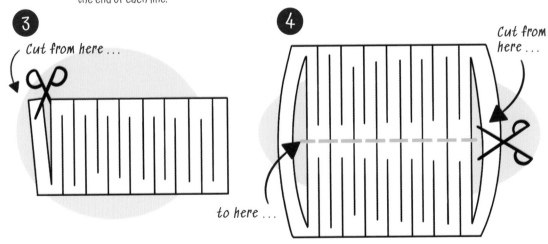

Cut from here ...

to here ...

5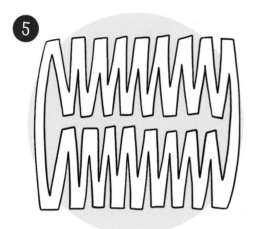

Carefully open out the postcard
to form a large loop...

6

...and step right through it!

What's going on?

The pattern of lines you cut into the postcard is basically a big, long zigzag. It cuts the card into a long, thin, continuous strip. If you made the lines closer together, the strip would be thinner, and even longer. How thin do you think you could make the strip, and how big could you make the loop, without it breaking apart? Give it a try! (If you have another spare postcard, that is.)

DRAW PERFECT CIRCLES

How can you draw a circle without a pair of compasses? Mathematics to the rescue!

The trick

Drawing a circle is useful for all kinds of art projects. You can also use this trick to draw part of a circle—for drawing a rainbow, for example.

All you need is a piece of paper, and a pencil. Hold the pencil as you would normally for writing. Then press down on the paper with the fingernail on your third finger.

Lift up the rest of your hand, so that just one fingertip and the pencil are touching the paper. Then, use your other hand to rotate the paper, while holding the pencil and your fingertip still. The pencil will draw a circle!

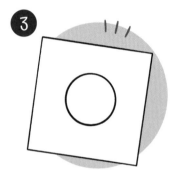

For a bigger circle, use your little finger, or your wrist.

What's going on?

Every point around the edge of a circle is the same distance from the middle. This distance is called the radius.

So, keeping a fixed distance between the pencil and your fingertip, and spinning the paper around your fingertip, produces a circle! A pair of compasses works this way, too.

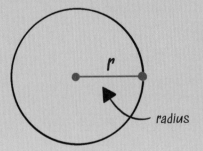

r

radius

DRAW PERFECT SPIRALS

Here's another crafty trick, this time for drawing a spiral.

the trick

First, use a ruler and pencil to draw a line of dots across your paper, all the same distance (such as 1 cm or ½ inch) apart.

2 Start at the middle dot, and draw a semicircle, or half-circle, to the next dot.

3 Now draw a bigger semicircle from that dot to the next unused dot in the other direction.

4 Continue drawing semicircles, to the next opposite dot until you have a spiral!

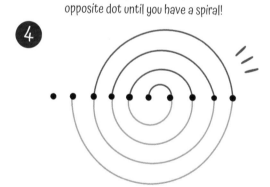

What's going on?

Hearts can be hard to draw, but mathematics is here to help!

Simply draw two circles, and a square, overlapping each other, like this:

Erase the parts you don't need, and there's your heart!

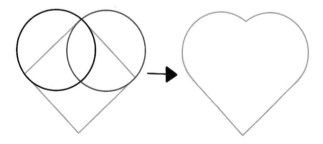

FIND THE VOLUME

Volume tells us the amount of space that a 3D object takes up. It wasn't always easy to figure out volume, until an amazing genius had a brilliant idea!

the trick

Finding the volume of a 3D shape is common in mathematics. It's quite easy for a regular, solid shape like a cube.

This cube is 3 cm tall, 3 cm wide, and 3 cm deep (from front to back).

To find the volume, you multiply together:

height x width x depth

3 cm x 3 cm x 3 cm
(That's about 1.2 x 1.2 x 1.2 inches.)

= 27 cm³, or 27 cubic cm. (1.65 cubic inches.)

But what about a more complicated shape that's really hard to measure? How do you find the volume of that?

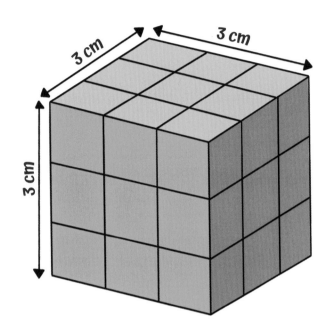

Around 2,200 years ago, this very problem was troubling ancient Greek inventor and scientist, Archimedes, as the king had asked him to find the volume of a golden crown.

According to legend, Archimedes took a bath. As he sank into the water, he saw the water level rise. "EUREKA" he yelled (ancient Greek for "I've got it!"). He'd solved the problem!

All he had to do was drop the crown into some water, and measure how much the water rose!

What's going on?

Archimedes realized that when he got into the bath, his body pushed some water out of the way—or "displaced" it.

If Archimedes filled a pot with water to the brim, then dropped in the crown, it would push some of the water over the edges. The amount of water it displaced would be the same volume as the crown itself. Then he could measure the volume of the water that had overflowed.

EUREKA!

TESSELLATE IT LIKE ESCHER

M. C. (or Maurits Cornelis) Escher was a famous Dutch artist who was inspired by mathematics.

His pictures include all kinds of illusions and shapes, especially tessellating shapes. These are shapes that fit together, or tessellate, so that you can use them to fill a space exactly.

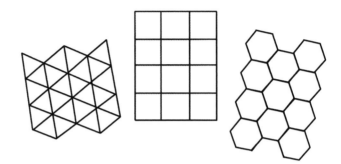

Many simple shapes tessellate . . .

But if you know how, you can copy Escher and create much more interesting ones, like these:

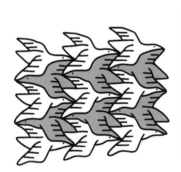

the trick

Here's how to design your own cool tessellating tiles . . .

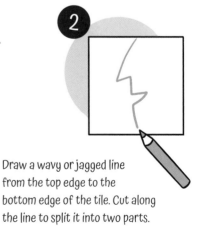

1

First, draw a basic square or rectangle on a piece of paper, using a ruler to make it neat and accurate. Use squared or graph paper if you have some. Cut out your shape to make a tile.

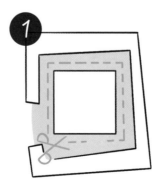

2

Draw a wavy or jagged line from the top edge to the bottom edge of the tile. Cut along the line to split it into two parts.

Swap the two parts around, and put the two straight edges together, like this.

3

Join the edges together with some tape. Then draw a line from left to right.

4

Cut along the line, and swap the two pieces around so that the flat edges touch.

5

Tape the finished shape together. Whatever shape you make in this way will tessellate!

6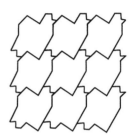

To draw a tessellating pattern, make a tessellating shape out of thick paper, and draw around it, as shown. With practice, you can use this method to make shapes that look like animals, letters, or other objects.

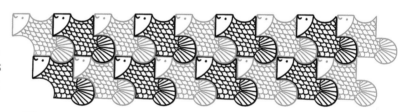

What's going on?

To tessellate, tiles have to fit together exactly. By cutting new edges and putting them on the outsides, you're giving one side of each tile a shape that will fit the other side of the next tile perfectly.

This is just the start—tessellating can get much more complicated! For example, can you make two different shapes that tessellate together in a pattern?

FRACTAL TREES

A fractal is a special type of mathematical pattern. You can keep adding to it by following the same simple rules ... which makes for some cool picture-making tricks!

the trick

This easy fractal is a good one to start with.

First, draw a tree trunk with two branches. Now, on each branch, draw two smaller branches. And on each of those smaller branches, draw two more even smaller branches ... and so on!

Before long, you've got a tree! You can then add fruit, leaves, birds, or whatever else you like.

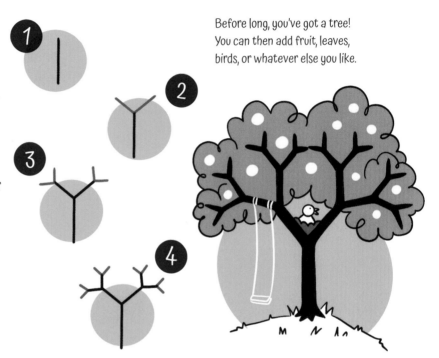

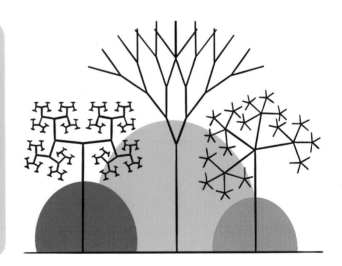

What's going on?

In a fractal, each part of the shape repeats the same pattern as the whole shape. If you had space, you could go on adding smaller and smaller bits forever!

You can change the rules, as long as you repeat them every time. What if you always add three branches? What if you put a circle at every joining point? There's no end to the patterns you can make ...

FRACTAL SNOWFLAKES

Here's another type of fractal that makes a snowflake–like shape.

the trick

Start with a basic equilateral triangle—a triangle in which all three sides are equal length. The rule for this fractal is: wherever there's a straight line, divide it into thirds, and draw another equilateral triangle on the middle third.

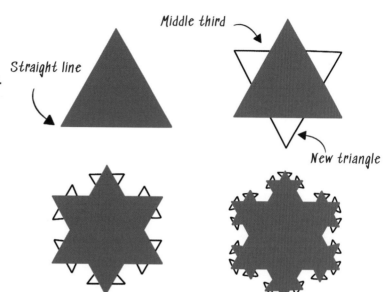

Straight line

Middle third

New triangle

ENDLESS TRIANGLES

And another—it's called a Sierpiński triangle. You could draw this one in green to look like a pine tree.

the trick

Draw a triangle that points upward, like this one:

Now draw an upside-down, smaller triangle inside it. Now you've created more triangles. Find all the upward-pointing triangles and draw smaller, upside-down triangles inside them ... And so on!

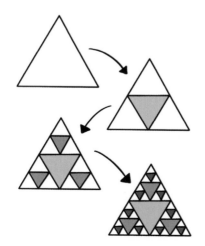

DOTS AND BOXES

This is more of a game than a trick—but you might be able to trick your opponent while you're playing it! You need two people, pens or pencils in different shades, and some graph paper.

the trick

First, draw a square of dots on the paper, using a marker or felt-tip pen so you can see them easily.
For your first game, don't make it too big—try a square that's 6 dots by 6 dots, like this.

graph paper

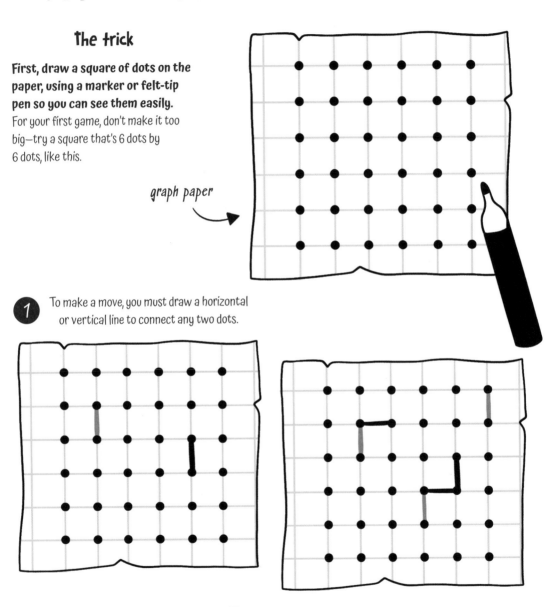

1 To make a move, you must draw a horizontal or vertical line to connect any two dots.

2 One player goes first, then you take turns. Each person adds a new line, connecting any two dots that haven't been joined already.

3 To score a point, you must complete a full square on the grid by drawing the last of its four sides, as shown. Whenever you manage to do this, shade in the box, and take an extra turn!

Keep taking turns until no one can draw any more lines, and all the boxes are completed. The winner is the person who has the most boxes!

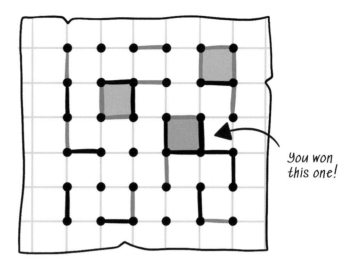

You won this one!

What's going on?

It sounds simple—and the rules ARE very simple. But you'll soon find yourself trying to find all kinds of sneaky ways to win, using mathematical problem-solving to calculate how many turns each person has left, and how to set yourself up to score points.

How can you play so that you'll get the chance to complete a box, and your opponent won't?

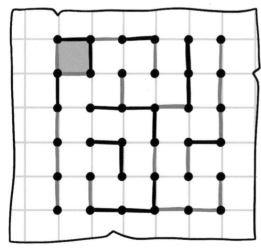

Can you set up a long "corridor," like this, so that you get to fill in lots of boxes all at once?

WHAT COMES NEXT?

Look at this row of numbers. Which number do you think comes next?

That probably wasn't too tricky, as it's a very simple number sequence. You just add two each time, so the next number is ... 15!

The trick

Here's another sequence to try. See if you can figure out what comes next, and then try it on a friend or relative.

Answer: First add 1, then add 2, then 3, and so on. So the next three numbers are ... 29–37–46

What about this sequence?

Answer: Each number in the sequence is the previous two numbers added together. So the next three numbers are ... 21–34–55

What's going on?

Mathematics has lots of sequences— times tables, for example. For each sequence, there's a simple rule. Once you know it, you can predict the next number. The last sequence on this page is called the Fibonacci sequence. It often pops up in the natural world. For example, flowers are likely to have a number of petals from the Fibonacci sequence, such as 5, 8, 13, or 21.

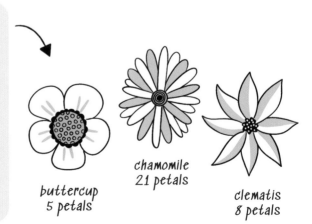

buttercup
5 petals

chamomile
21 petals

clematis
8 petals

SQUARES AND SPIRALS

There's a trick for drawing a spiral on page 23, but you can use Fibonacci numbers to draw another kind of spiral.

The trick

You'll need a piece of graph or squared paper, a pencil, and a ruler.

First, draw a box 1 square across—this is the 1 in the Fibonacci sequence. 1

Then draw another single square next to it. 1

Then a square box, 2 squares across, above them. 2

Then a square box, 3 squares across. 3

 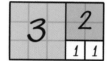

Keep following the sequence to draw bigger and bigger boxes. You'll find each box fits perfectly next to the previous ones, until it looks like this . . . :

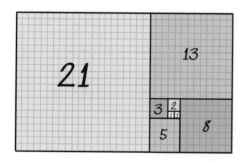

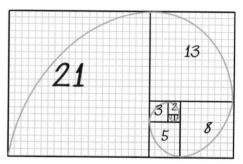

To draw the spiral, connect the corners of the boxes together in sequence, with a curved line.

Did you know?

This spiral appears in nature, too!

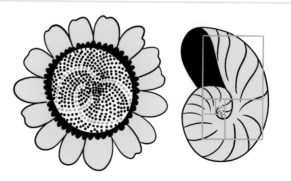

TRIANGLE TRICKS

Here's another mystery mathematical sequence. Can you tell what comes next?

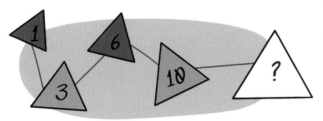

You may have spotted this pattern:

Add 2	Add 3	Add 4	Add 5
1	**3**	**6**	**10**	__

So the next number is 15. But there's a bit more to this sequence. These aren't just numbers—they're triangular numbers!

The trick

A triangular number is a number that can be arranged into a triangle. To test this out, you need lots of coins, buttons, or counters that are all the same size. Put them on a table top, and start making triangles!

1
3
6
10

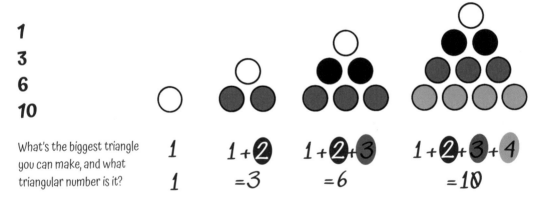

What's the biggest triangle you can make, and what triangular number is it?

1

1

$1 + 2$

$= 3$

$1 + 2 + 3$

$= 6$

$1 + 2 + 3 + 4$

$= 10$

What's going on?

Every time you make a bigger triangle, you need to add an extra row of coins (or other items) at the bottom. And each time, you need one more item in that row. That's why triangular numbers go up by increasing numbers.

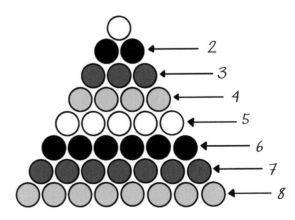

FLIP IT!

Now you've got your head around triangle numbers, here's a triangular trick.
Challenge a friend to do it, then show them how!

The trick

People can spend ages puzzling over this, but it's actually simple!

? ?

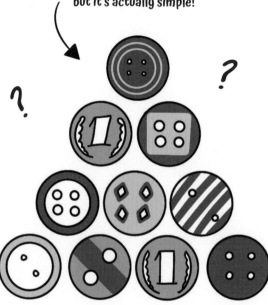

Arrange 10 counters or buttons to make a triangle, like this.

The challenge is to turn the triangle upside down by moving only 3 circles.

Just move each point of the triangle to the opposite side. Ta-da!

Did you know?

You can experiment with your counters to make other shape numbers, too.

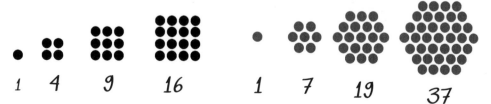

1   4   9   16   1   7   19   37

Square numbers, for example ...   and hexagonal numbers!

PUZZLING PASCAL

These two tricks go together. To get the second one to work, you have to get the first one right! It's another triangle teaser, known as Pascal's triangle.

The trick

Here's a triangle made up of 16 rows of boxes. We've filled in some of the numbers for you—but can you fill in the rest? You're going to need a calculator! Copy the shape onto a piece of paper, then write in the numbers.

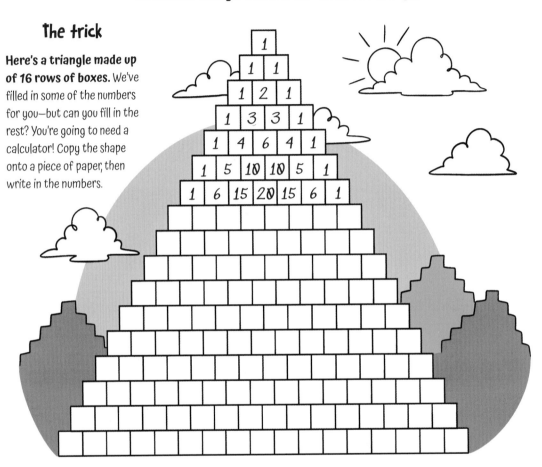

What's going on?

Did you figure it out? Once you know how it works, it's easy to complete the triangle. The number in each box is made of the two numbers above it added together.

If there's only one number above it, because it's at the side, then it's the same as that number. That's why there are 1s all the way down both sides!

The triangle is named after Blaise Pascal, a French mathematician who lived in the 1600s.

PASCAL'S PATTERNS

Look more closely at Pascal's triangle, and you'll find it's full of patterns.

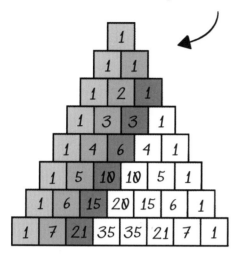

If you follow the second diagonal row down the side, you'll see it follows the main number sequence.

And look at the third diagonal row. Is that sequence familiar? It's the triangular numbers!

There are more patterns hidden in there, too. Try it!

Try this!

Take the Pascal's triangle you filled in, and a dark marker or felt-tip pen. Now simply shade in all the boxes with odd numbers in them. What happens?

What's going on?

Hang on, have you seen that pattern somewhere before?
Well, you have if you've read page 29! It's the Sierpiński triangle fractal pattern. Proof that in mathematics, everything is interrelated!

Hi Grandpa, I'm just checking in ...

PICK A CARD ...

A symmetrical shape is exactly the same on both sides, like this butterfly.

The mirror line divides the shape into equal halves.

But this Z shape has a different type of symmetry—rotational symmetry. That means you can rotate it into a different position that looks the same.

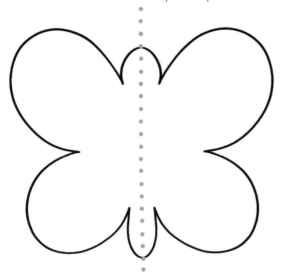

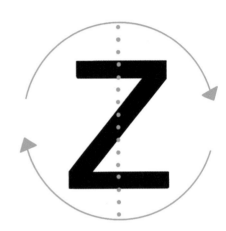

Symmetry is important to patterns, and you can use rotational symmetry to do an amazing mathematical magic trick.

The trick

Spread out a pack of cards, and find which ones have rotational symmetry.
For example, a Queen does, as well as nearly all the Diamond cards—they are the same both ways up!

Remove the cards that DO have rotational symmetry, and keep only the ones that DON'T. Arrange them so that they are all the "right" way up (with more of the symbols the right way up than not).

This 2 of Hearts DOES have rotational symmetry, but the 3 of Hearts DOES NOT.

Now to play the trick! Shuffle the pack (making sure you keep the cards the same way around), and hold them face-down. Ask a friend or relative to pick one and look at it without showing you, then put it back in the pack. While they are looking at it, sneakily turn the pack the other way around.

After they've put their card back in, you can shuffle the pack again. Then spread the cards out and study them carefully. The one that's upside down is the one they picked! Pull it out of the pack dramatically, and say, "Abracadabra!"

What's going on?

Playing cards are designed to be easy to read either way up. So people usually assume they all look exactly the same either way up, and all have rotational symmetry. In fact, many of them don't, but most people don't notice!

COG CONUNDRUM

A cog or gear is a wheel with a regular pattern of sticking-out "teeth" all the way around the edge.

Why? So that it can lock into another cog. When one cog turns, so does the next one, as the teeth push it around.

Cogs are an important part of many machines, and engineers have to use mathematics to make sure they work properly!

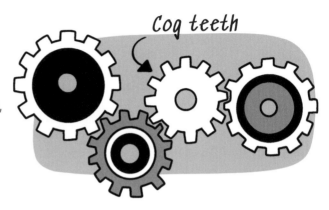

Cog teeth

The trick

Tests and exams often include brain-bending cog or gear puzzles, like this one.

Can you figure out which way the last cog will turn? Try it—and see how long it takes you.

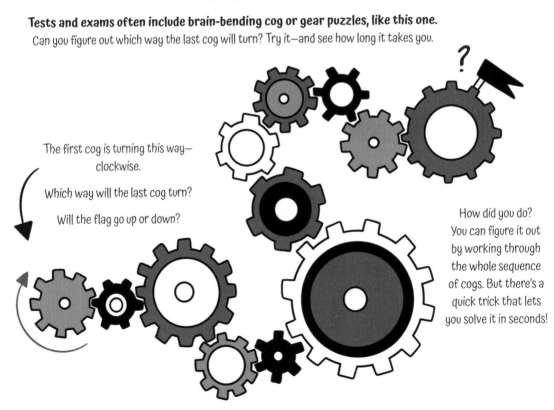

The first cog is turning this way— clockwise.

Which way will the last cog turn?

Will the flag go up or down?

How did you do? You can figure it out by working through the whole sequence of cogs. But there's a quick trick that lets you solve it in seconds!

What's going on?

So what's the trick?

Just count the cogs! Each cog moves in the opposite direction from the one before it.

So if the first cog turns clockwise, the second cog must turn counterclockwise (or anti-clockwise).

Then the third cog turns clockwise . . .

The fourth cog turns counterclockwise (or anti-clockwise) . . . and so on.

If the cogs in the chain add up to an EVEN number, the last one will turn in the OPPOSITE direction from the first one.

If they add up to an ODD number, the last one will turn in the SAME direction as the first one.

Simple!

In our puzzle, there are 12 cogs— an even number.

So the last cog turns the opposite way from the first one: counterclockwise . . . and the flag goes up!

CLEVER CODES

This paper code wheel helps you send uncrackable coded messages to your friends—with the help of numbers!

The trick

To make the wheel, draw and cut out two paper circles, one about 10 cm across (4 inches), and one about 8 cm (3 inches) across. With the smaller circle on top, pin them together in the middle, using a metal paper fastener.

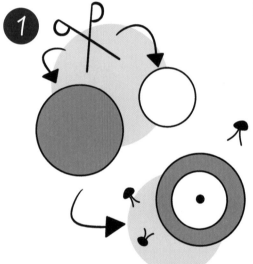

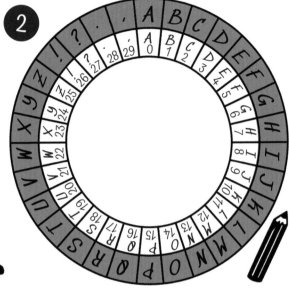

Use a ruler and pencil to draw 30 equal boxes around the edge of each circle, as above. (If it's a bit tricky, you could trace our wheel.) Fill in the outer one with the letters of the alphabet, plus punctuation marks, and the inner wheel with the alphabet, plus punctuation marks, and the numbers 0 to 29, as above.

To make a code, choose a number from the wheel as your encryption key. Turn the inner wheel so that your number lines up with A on the outer wheel.

For example, if you choose 19, line up 19 on the inner wheel with A on the outer wheel.

Keeping the wheel in this position, use it to encode your message. Find each letter of your message on the outer wheel, and use the letter under it instead.

For example, A becomes T, B becomes U, and so on.

So this message:
THE BAT FLIES TONIGHT

Becomes this coded message:
MAX UTM YEBXL MHGBZAM

To read the message, the other person just needs their own code wheel, and the information about which number you used.

What's going on?

Any time you want to encode a message, you can choose a different encryption key number— so your code is different every time!

Codes can be guessed by studying the patterns of letters and words. But changing the code every time makes this much harder.

ZEROS AND ONES

Binary is the number system that computers use to store information. It can record numbers, letters, pictures, and other information as patterns of 0s and 1s.

How does binary work?

We normally count using a system called Base 10, which contains these symbols: 0, 1, 2, 3, 4, 5, 6, 7, 8, 9. We can count higher than 9 by using places. Each place represents a number ten times larger than the place to its right.

| 0 | 1 | 2 | 3 | 4 | 5 | 6 | 7 | 8 | 9 |

| 10 | 11 |

In this place, "1" means 1.

In this place, "1" actually represents 10.

In binary, you only have two symbols: 0 and 1. Each place represents a number twice as large as the place to its right.

Base 10	Binary
1	1
2	10
3	11
4	100
5	101
6	110
7	111
8	1000

What's going on?

In binary, the 1000s, 100, 10s, and 1s are the same as our 8s, 4s, 2s, and 1s.

So 15, for example, is 1111. It has . . .

One 8   One 4   One 2   One 1

Can you convert your age into binary?

BINARY CODE

How can a great big long string of 0s and 1s contain a coded message? Read on to find out!

The trick

You need some graph or squared paper, a pen or pencil, and a ruler. First, draw a box 20 squares wide by 20 squares high. Draw your picture message inside it by shading in squares to create an image, as shown. (Keep it simple!)

Starting at the top left, work your way along each row in turn, adding a 0 in each empty square, and a *1* in each shaded square.

Then, on another piece of paper, write a list of the 0s and 1s, as they appear in the square.

You'll be left with a long list that appears totally random! It might look something like this...

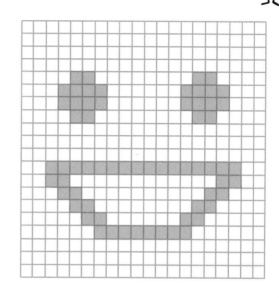

0000000000000000000000000000000000000000000011011011011011100000111110100100010000001
01010110110 0100000 ...

What's going on?

To decode the message, the other person just has to know the size of box you used. They get your list of 0s and 1s, and copy it into their own 20 x 20 box. When they shade the squares with a 1 in them, the picture message will appear!

THE MISSING MONEY

Various versions of this famous mathematical mystery have been boggling people's minds for years!
Read the story, and see if you can figure it out. Then try it on your friends.

The trick

Three friends are on a camping trip to Yellowstone Park, sharing one tent. When they arrive, the owner charges them $30 to stay for one night.
So the friends each pay $10.

Later, the owner realizes that she charged them too much, as the price is actually $25.
She sends her assistant with $5 in dollar bills to take back to the friends.

When the assistant gives the friends their $5 back, they realize they can't split the bills equally between them. So they take one each, and give the assistant the other two as a tip.

So each friend has paid $9
(they each paid $10 and got $1 back).

That totals $27.

And they gave $2 to the assistant.

That makes $29.

WHERE'S THE OTHER $1 GONE?

What's going on?

Stumped? This sneaky trick might fool you, but there is a solution. The reason it doesn't make sense is that you're trying to add up the wrong things:

The $27 the friends paid in total . . . and the $2 tip.

If you think about it, if the friends got $3 back, $27 must have gone to the campsite.

$25 to the owner . . .

. . . and $2 to the assistant.

The $2 shouldn't be added to the $27—it's already part of it!
Instead, the $27 should be added to the $3 change—making $30 in total.

Did you know?

If you're stuck with a puzzling problem like this—in class or in real life—it can help to "locate" all the numbers. Think about WHERE each amount has ended up.

$25—with the owner . . .

$2—with the assistant . . .

$3—returned to the friends.

THE INFINITE HOTEL

One of the strangest ideas in mathematics is infinity. Numbers are infinite, meaning that they go on forever. Whatever the biggest number you can think of is, you can always add 1!

the trick

You've just arrived in Numberopolis, and need somewhere to stay—but all the hotels are full. Your friend, Professor Polygon, tells you to try the Infinite Hotel.

Clever mathematicians write "infinity" using this symbol:

It's an endless loop, so it goes on forever!

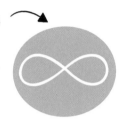

Now try this puzzle . . .

The Infinite Hotel has an infinite number of rooms. But it's full, as it also has an infinite number of guests. However, the hotel manager says you're in luck— you can have a room!

How is he going to manage that?

What's going on?

The manager doesn't have any empty rooms. But as he has infinite rooms, he can just move everyone up.

He asks the guest in room 1 to move to room 2, the guest in room 2 to move to room 3, and so on, up to infinity. Now you can have room 1!

ACHILLES AND THE TORTOISE

Here's another infinity-related mind-boggler.

The trick

One day, a tortoise challenged ancient Greek hero, Achilles, to a race . . . if she could have a head start. So Achilles agreed she could start 10 paces in front.

But when Achilles caught up to where the tortoise had started, she'd moved ahead.

And when he caught up to THAT point, she'd moved ahead again!

In fact, even though the distance got smaller and smaller, Achilles could never catch up!

What's going on?

This seems to PROVE that Achilles can never catch the tortoise. Yet we all know he can! Runners overtake each other all the time.

So what's wrong?

Achilles could try to catch the tortoise an infinite number of times. But the distance gets shorter each time, until it's infinitely short, and Achilles is infinitely slow.

But infinitely short amounts of space and time can't exist in the real world—they're just ideas. And Achilles wouldn't actually slow down. Instead, we measure speed by how much distance you cover in a given time. Looking at it that way, Achilles would win!

MINDBOGGLING MYSTERIES OF MÖBIUS

How many sides does a piece of paper have? Two, you say? Well, this cool trick makes a piece of paper with only one side. All you need to amaze your friends is a big piece of paper, scissors, glue or tape, and a pencil.

The trick

Cut a long strip of paper, about 20 cm long (8 inches) and 3 cm (1.2 inches) wide.

Make a loop in the strip and hold the ends in front of you. Flip one end over to make a half-twist.

Tape or glue the ends together. You'll have a loop with a twist in it, called a Möbius strip.

Your Möbius strip may not seem strange, but it is. Don't believe it? Draw a line along the middle of the strip until you get back to where you started. You've drawn on both sides! Or rather one side, as there IS only one!

Next, carefully cut along the line you've just drawn, until you get back to where you started. You're cutting the strip in half, right? WRONG! There's still only one strip!

To cut a Möbius strip in two, make a new one and mark a point $1/3$ of the way across. Draw a line starting from that point, staying $1/3$ of the way across the strip all the way around. Now cut along that line. Ta-da!

What's going on?

A Möbius strip involves some weird and wonderful mathematics. When you flip over the end of the strip, and join the ends, you are making a single, continuous surface, with only one edge. When you cut the strip along the middle, the strip's original single edge becomes one edge of a new, longer strip with two edges.

However, you're doing something different in the second experiment. As you cut off the edge of the strip, you create a longer loop, but the middle of the strip gets left behind. It's still a Möbius strip, just narrower!

MÖBIUS HEARTS

Now for a trick involving two Möbius strips! Perfect for number-lovers on Valentine's Day …

The trick

First, make two Möbius strips. For each one, cut a strip of paper about 20 cm (8 inches) long, and 2–3 cm (about 1 inch) wide. Curl it into a loop, flip over one end to make a half-twist, then tape the two ends together.

Tape together the two loops at right angles, and on both sides. Now snip into the middle of one strip with some pointy scissors, and start cutting lengthways. Keep cutting until you end up where you started.

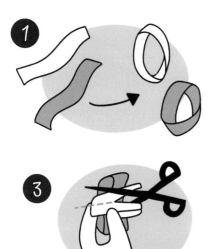

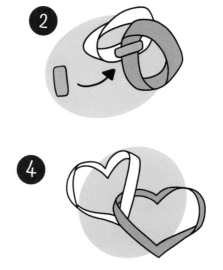

The strips will separate into two hearts, linked together!

What's going on?

As you'll know if you read pages 50-51, cutting a Möbius strip in half lengthways results in one big loop. That's because a Möbius strip only has one edge.

But two Möbius strips have two edges. By joining them together and then cutting them, you get two separate objects. The twist creates the heart shapes!

SAM'S SOCK DRAWER

Sam's a brilliant mathematician, but he's not very good at keeping his sock drawer tidy.
Can you help him find a matching pair?

the trick

Sam's sock drawer contains four white socks, five pink socks, eight orange socks, and 12 black socks.

Sam wants a matching pair of socks, but it's too dark to see. How many socks should he pull out at once to make sure he has a matching pair?

This question stumps most people, and they usually say a number that's much too high.

The answer is actually . . . 5!

What's going on?

Imagine Sam pulled out 4 socks in the dark.
They could be white, pink, orange, and black,
so no matching pairs.

But he only needs to pull out one more, and it will match one of them!

THE POTATO PERCENTAGE PUZZLER

Try this percentage puzzle on anyone who thinks they are smart! Watch how many of them think it's easy and give you their answer in a flash! (The WRONG answer, of course.)

The trick

Farmer Palmer has a sack containing 100 kg of potatoes, freshly picked from his field.

The potatoes are mostly water, like many vegetables. In fact, they are 99% water.

You could think of these as 100 pounds of potatoes, if you prefer. The unit isn't important.

Farmer Palmer leaves the sack of potatoes in a shed for a few days, and they start to dry out. After a while, they are only 98% water.

Now, how much do the potatoes weigh?

If you came up with an answer of 99 kg or thereabouts, then you're like most people!

But it's not the right answer. The right answer is . . . 50 kg.

What's going on?

This puzzle trips people up because they make a mistake. When they hear that 99% water has become 98% water, they think that 1 kg of water has gone, so the weight is 1 kg less.

Instead, you need to think about it like this:

At first, the potatoes are 99% water, weighing 99 kg.

The rest must be 1% non-water stuff, weighing 1 kg.

Later, the potatoes are 98% water. The non-water stuff must be 2% of the total weight.

But they still only weigh 1 kg.

2% is the same as $1/50$, and 1 kg is $1/50$ of 50 kg. Not 99 kg!

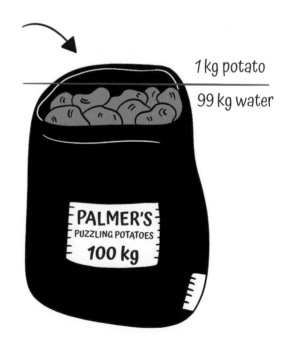

1 kg potato

99 kg water

PALMER'S
PUZZLING POTATOES
100 kg

IMPOSSIBLE PAPER

Tell a friend you've got an impossible piece of paper, and they'll be desperate to see it!

The trick

1 **Take a normal piece of paper.** Fold it in half lengthways, then open it out again.

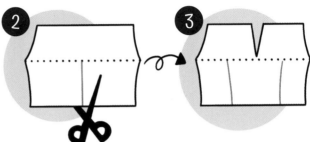

2 With one side toward you, cut into the middle of the paper, up to the fold.

3 Turn the paper around so you have the opposite edge toward you.

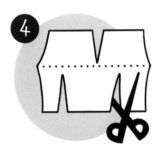

4 Make two cuts up to the fold, like this.

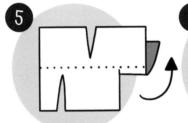

5 Now take the right-hand end of the paper, and fold the back flap over toward you, and the front flap under, and away from you, so they switch places.

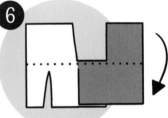

6 Take the flap in the middle, and fold it so that it sticks up.

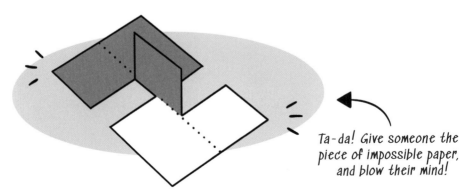

Ta-da! Give someone the piece of impossible paper, and blow their mind!

TURN A PIECE OF PAPER INSIDE OUT!

While you're doing impossible things with paper, why not turn a piece of paper inside out?

the trick

Take a normal piece of paper, or a page torn out of an old magazine.

Fold it in half lengthways, open it out, then fold over the ends to the middle fold. Open it out and fold it the same way in the other direction. The folds will make a box shape in the middle of the paper. Use a ruler and a pen to draw a cross in the box.

Cut carefully along both lines of the cross. Now fold back the ends of the paper, then the sides. Open out the triangle-shaped flaps and fold them back, too. Open out the rectangular flaps ... you've turned the paper inside out!

What's going on?

This trick looks amazing, but it's not actually that strange. As long as the hole in the paper is big enough to let the folded edges pass through, it's easy!

Did you know?

This trick looks best if the paper is different on different sides. So a page from a magazine is perfect—or try a piece of newspaper with a different design on each side.

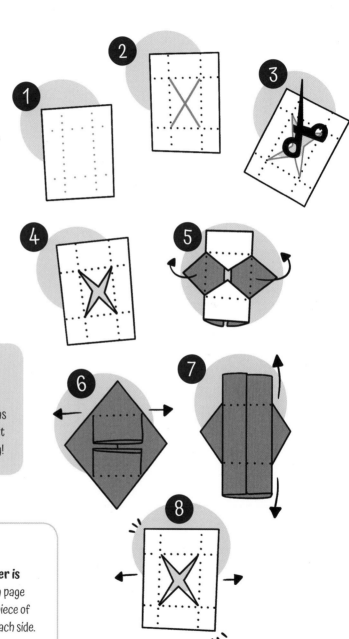

57

THE THREE-DOORS DILEMMA

This well-known mind-boggler used to be part of a famous game show!

The trick

You are given a choice of three doors. One of them has the star prize behind it—a car. The other two have goats behind them. You want to pick the prize door!

You pick a door. But instead of opening it, the game-show host opens a different door, revealing a goat.

Now you have another choice. Do you stick with your first choice, or switch to the other closed door? Which gives you the best chance?

If you think sticking with your choice is best—wrong! If you think it doesn't matter because they both have the same chance—wrong again! But why?

What's going on?

Most people say it makes no difference, as all the doors have an equal ⅓ chance of being right.
But that's not how it works!

When you choose a door, there's a ⅓ chance it's right.

There's a ⅔ chance it's behind one of the other two doors.

When one of the other doors is opened, there's still a ⅓ chance it's behind your door . . .

. . . and a ⅔ chance it's behind one of the other two.

You now know that one of those two other doors has a goat behind it, so it can't be that one. So there's now a ⅔ chance it's behind the other one!

Did you know?

The real-life show proved this was true. People won more often if they switched.

You can set up the game yourself with 3 paper cups, and little pictures of a car and two goats. Test it on a friend and see what happens!

UP AND DOWN THE MOUNTAIN

This brain-bending puzzle will probably confuse anyone you share it with.
But they'll be even more befuddled when they hear the answer!

the trick

Professor Probable decides to go on a two-day hike with her dog, Random.

They set off at 8 a.m. in the morning, and walk all the way up a mountain. They camp at the top overnight.
The next morning, at 8 a.m., they begin walking back down the same path.

On the way down, the professor looks at her watch and says to Random: "Wow! It's 12.30 p.m., and we're at the exact same spot as we were at 12.30 p.m. yesterday!"

The question is, could that happen? What are the chances that you could find yourself at the exact same place at the exact same time of day on the way down, as on the way up? Do you think it's likely, or unlikely?

The answer may surprise you.
The truth is, it's not just likely—it's guaranteed. You might not notice it like the professor did, but at some point, it has to happen! But why?

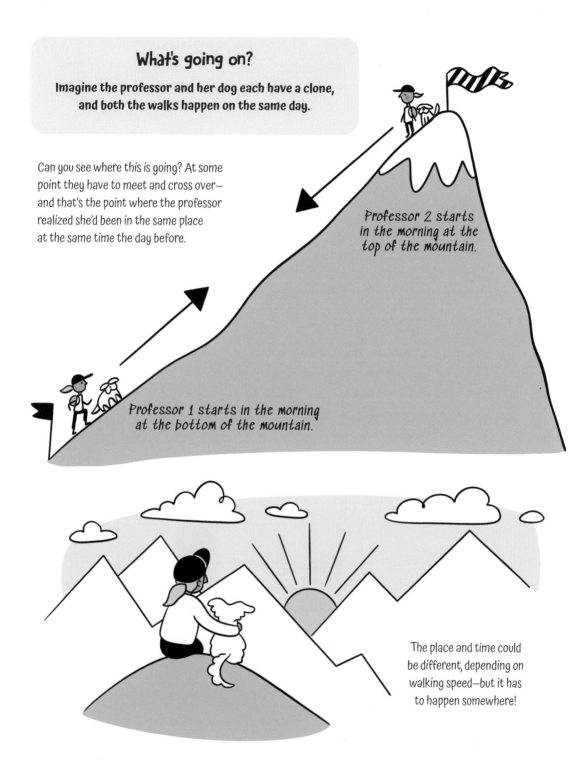

What's going on?

Imagine the professor and her dog each have a clone, and both the walks happen on the same day.

Can you see where this is going? At some point they have to meet and cross over—and that's the point where the professor realized she'd been in the same place at the same time the day before.

Professor 2 starts in the morning at the top of the mountain.

Professor 1 starts in the morning at the bottom of the mountain.

The place and time could be different, depending on walking speed—but it has to happen somewhere!

THE RICE RIDDLER

If you were the king in this story, would you make the same mistake?

the trick

Long ago, according to an old legend, a wise man invented the game of chess.
The king loved the new game so much, he offered the inventor any reward he asked for.

The inventor said he would like some rice. He asked the king to give him one grain of rice for the first square of the chessboard, two grains for the next square, four for the next square, eight for the next square, and so on, doubling the amount each time, until all the squares on the board were used up.

The king agreed, as that didn't sound like very much rice. But he was wrong!

What's going on?

There are 64 squares on a chessboard, so the amount of rice would have to double 63 times.
The first eight squares would look like this:

1	2	4	8	16	32	64	128

1	2	4	8	16	32	64	128
256	512	1,024	2,048	4,096	8,192	16,384	32,768

While the next eight squares would look like this:

You'd pass a million grains of rice at square 21, and 100 million at square 28. In total, all the rice for each square would add up to 18,446,744,073,709,551,615. That's more than 18 million trillion grains of rice—enough to cover all the land in the world with rice! As the king discovered, numbers grow incredibly fast when you keep doubling them.

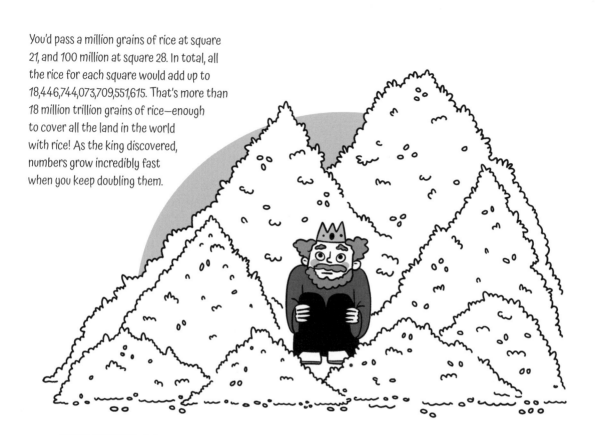

Did you know?

This type of rapid increase by doubling is called exponential growth. It's very important in mathematics, and in real life, too. For example, populations of living things can grow like this in some situations.

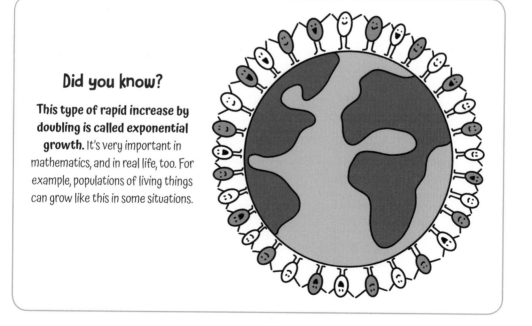

PAPER-FOLDING CHALLENGE

Here's another exponential growth trick. Can you fold a piece of paper in half eight times? (Without unfolding it after each fold, that is ...) Challenge a friend to do it, or try it yourself.

The trick

Start with a simple piece of paper.

Fold it in half ... Then in half again ... And again, until you've folded it eight times. Did you manage it? Or was it a bit too difficult?

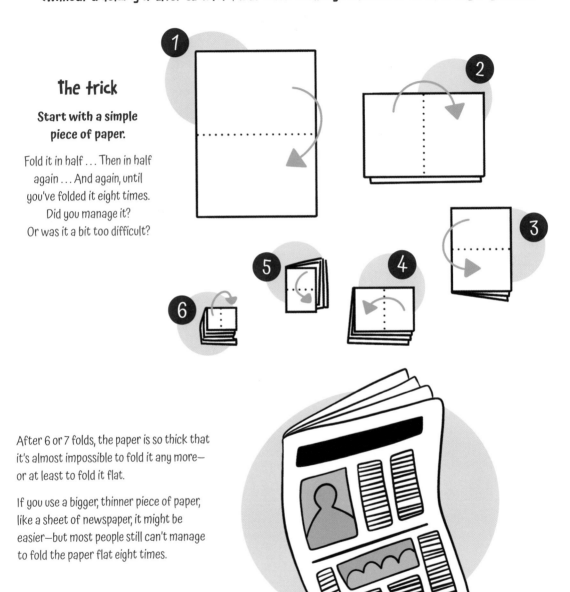

After 6 or 7 folds, the paper is so thick that it's almost impossible to fold it any more—or at least to fold it flat.

If you use a bigger, thinner piece of paper, like a sheet of newspaper, it might be easier—but most people still can't manage to fold the paper flat eight times.

What's going on?

Every time you fold the paper, it doubles in thickness by exponential growth—just like the rice grains on page 62. So by the time you do the 7th fold, you're trying to fold a pile of paper that's 64 sheets thick, and very small. If you manage that, the paper is 128 sheets thick, and even smaller, when you try to do the eighth fold.

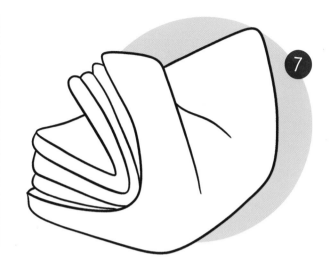

Did you know?

Some people HAVE managed to fold paper up to 10, 11 or 12 times, by using a giant piece of very thin paper. So it's not impossible. But you couldn't go much further, because of how thick the paper would get. If you could fold it 42 times, for example, the stack of paper would be thick enough to reach to the Moon!

MAGIC SQUARES

Long ago, the legends say, a turtle walked out of China's great Yellow River. On its back was a strange pattern of dots, showing nine numbers in a square. All the rows, columns, and diagonals in the square added up to 15.

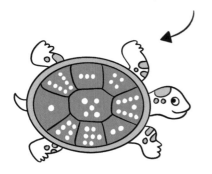

This is now called a magic square. Can you see how they work?

8	3	4
1	5	9
6	7	2

The trick

This is the magic square from the story. First, check the numbers add up to 15 in every direction.

Now see if you can solve the next square. It works the same way, but the arrangement of numbers is different.

What numbers should go where to make another square that adds up to 15 in every direction?

		4
		3
6		8

Can you create a magic square from nothing, starting with an empty grid?

What's going on?

There are actually several ways to make a 3x3 magic square. There are bigger magic squares, too, with 4x4 or 5x5 grids.

15	10	3	6
4	5	16	9
14	11	2	7
1	8	13	12

In this square, the numbers add up to 34 in all directions.

There's a trick for making a 3x3 magic square.

Start in the middle space at the top, and write a 1.

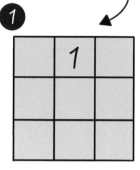

If the space you need to use is full, use the one below it, and continue on.

When the square is full, see if it worked! It doesn't work for a 4x4 square, because there's no middle space. Does it work for 5x5?

Now continue writing the numbers up to 9, always putting the next number one space up, and one to the right. If you're at the edge of the square, move to the opposite side, like this:

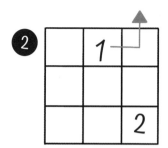

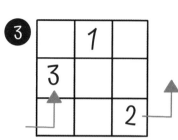

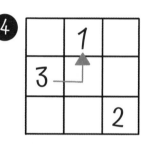

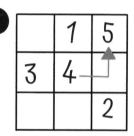

MAGIC TRIANGLES

Magic triangles exist, too!
Can you solve this one?
All the sides should add up to 19.

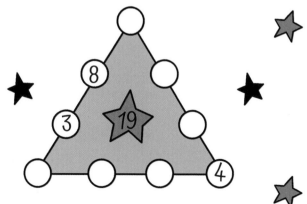

MAGIC STARS

How about a magic star?
Fill it in with the numbers 1 to 12.
Every straight line should add up to 26.

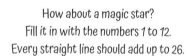

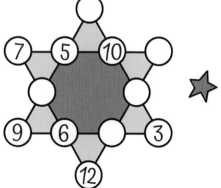

MAGICAL MATHEMATICAL MATCHES

These tricks combine mathematics with matches! Challenge your friends to see if they can solve them, before you reveal the answer. You don't need real matches—you can just draw the answers on paper, or cut out little strips of card to use as matches.

the tricks . . .

MAKE IT RIGHT

Here's a horribly wrong equation made up of matches. All you have to do is move one match into a different position, to make it correct. There are actually two ways to do it!

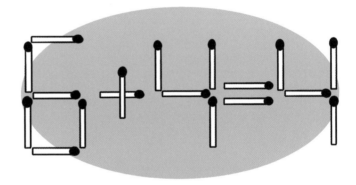

TRICKY TRIANGLES

For this trick, you must move three matches so that you end up with five triangles.

Take the third triangle, made up of three matches, and move it underneath the first two to make one big triangle, with four smaller ones inside it.

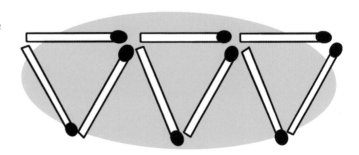

SEVEN SQUARES

Here's a pattern of four squares made using 12 matches. But you want seven squares! Move just two matches to make seven squares in total.

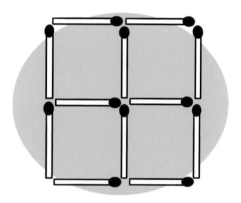

WHERE'S THE SQUARE?

This is the sneakiest trick of them all. Move one match to make a square.

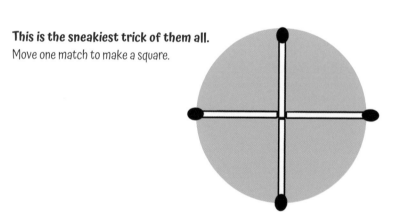

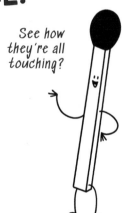

See how they're all touching?

Answers:

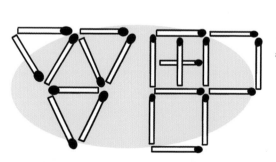

WHERE'S THE SQUARE
Move the top match up very slightly to leave a tiny square in the middle.
No one said it had to be a big square!

TRICKY TRIANGLES

SEVEN SQUARES

MAKE IT RIGHT
You could move the vertical match from the plus sign, turning it into a minus sign, and add the match to the 6 to turn it into an 8.

$8 - 4 = 4$

OR, you could take the match in the middle of the 6, and move it to turn the 6 into a 0.

$0 + 4 = 4$

MAGIC MINDREADING

Amaze your friends with these magnificent magic tricks. Of course, they're not really magic, but mathematics! (You might want to rehearse them a few times first.)

HIDDEN COINS

the trick

Ask a friend to select a few coins, and keep them in their hand so you can't see them.

Tell them you just need to ask a few simple questions, and you'll guess how much money there is.

First, ask them to add up the value of the coins. For example, these coins would add up to 75.

Next, ask your friend to do these steps. (They might need a calculator.)

- Double the amount
- Add 3
- Multiply the result by 5
- Take away 6 . . .

    and tell you the answer!

All you have to do is take away the last digit, and that's the amount of money!

For example, if the total was 75 . . .

Double it	= 150
Add 3	= 153
Multiply by 5	= 765
Subtract 6	= 759
Take off the last digit	= 75!

SECRET NUMBERS

This trick works in a similar way, but lets you guess someone's age AND their shoe size!

Ask the person to do these things, using a calculator:

- Think of their age
- Multiply it by 20
- Add on today's date
  (for example, if it's the 11th of June, add 11)
- Multiply the result by 5.
- Add on their shoe size.
- Take away 5 times today's date.
- Show you the answer.

The answer should give you their age followed by their shoe size!

For example, imagine they are 9 and wear size 3 shoes . . . the result will be 903.

Age: 9.

Shoe size: 3.

PECULIAR PREDICTIONS

With these tricks, you're not just going to guess numbers—
you'll actually predict the numbers IN ADVANCE. Sneaky, huh?

AND THE NUMBER IS ...

Before you start, write the number 5 on a piece of paper, fold it up, and hide it somewhere, like inside a book.

Tell your friend you're going to guess what number they're thinking of. Here's what they have to do:

First, think of a number. (It can be any number, but keeping it small will make it easier for them to solve the problems.)

- Double it.

- Add 10

- Divide the result by 2

- Subtract the number you first thought of.

Now tell them you know what number they've ended up with. Ask them to look for the piece of paper in the place where you hid it. They'll be amazed when they open it up and find the number that's inside their head!

What's going on?

How does it work? The answer is always 5!
The calculations always add up to the number they thought of, plus 5. So when they subtract their number, they always get 5.

72

THE 37 TRICK

Here's another super-simple number trick that appears magical!

The trick

Grab a pencil and paper, and a willing volunteer.
They'll probably need a calculator, too, as the trick requires some long division.

Ask your friend to write a 3-digit number on the paper, where the same number is repeated three times. For example, 333. Your friend should hide the paper from you to prove you're not cheating!

Now ask them to add each of the three digits together to find a sum:

3 + 3 + 3 = 9

Next, they should divide their original 3-digit number by the smaller sum total. Give them a minute or two to work this out!

333 ÷ 9 = 37

As long as your friend followed the instructions correctly, their answer will always be 37!

THE 1,089 TRICK

Here's another trick where you can always predict the answer ... because it's always 1,089!

1 456

2 456 654

3 198

The trick

Ask a friend to pick a 3-digit number, in which all the digits are different.

Now ask them to flip their number, making two mirror image numbers.

With a calculator, ask them to subtract the smaller number from the bigger number.

4 198 891

5 1089

Next, they should flip the answer, making two more mirror image numbers.

Finally, add those two numbers together.

To amaze your friend, show them the number 1,089, which you've sneakily hidden!

What's going on?

The number 1,089 has several special qualities. It's a square number (33 x 33) and it's also a "reverse-divisible number." If you reverse it, making 9,801, the result is divisible by 1,089.

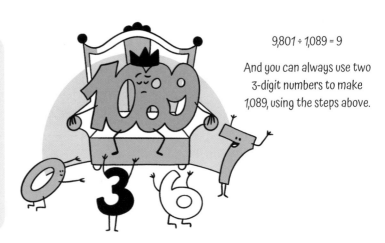

9,801 ÷ 1,089 = 9

And you can always use two 3-digit numbers to make 1,089, using the steps above.

THE 7–11–13 TRICK

This trick makes you look lightning-fast at mental calculations! Have a pen and paper ready.

The trick

Ask your friend to think of any 3-digit number, and tell you what it is.

Tell them you're going to ask them to do some calculations using a calculator, while you try to do them in your head. Ask your friend to multiply their number by 7, then 11, then 13.

But as they're doing it, simply write down the number they told you, repeated.

So, if their number was 983, write "983,983".

Shout "Done!" and show them the paper. It will be the right answer!

What's going on?

This baffling trick is simpler than it looks: 7 x 11 x 13 = 1,001.

And if you multiply any number by 1,001, you get 1,000 times that number, plus 1 x the number:

983 x 1,000 = 983,000

+

983 x 1 = 983

= 983,983

75

COIN FLIPPER

This trick really does look like magic!

The trick

Sit at a table and ask your friends to blindfold you.
Then ask them to put 12 coins on the table, and tell you
how many are heads.

Explain that you will arrange the coins, without
seeing them, into two groups, both with the same
number of heads.

All you have to do is remember the number of heads,
and move that number of coins into a separate group.
Then flip over all the coins in that group. (Shuffle the
coins around to hide what you're doing.) Ta-da!
Both groups will have the same number of heads!

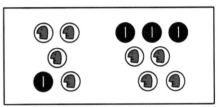

What's going on?

It seems amazing, but it's
simple mathematics.

Imagine 3 of the 12
coins are heads.

Move 3 coins into a
separate group.

If they're all heads,
the other group must
have no heads. When
you flip them, they'll be
all tails, matching the
other group.

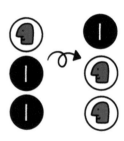

If you've got 1 head and
2 tails, that means the other
group must have 2 heads.
Flip your 3 coins, and they'll
have 2 heads as well!

However many coins are
heads, it always works.
Try it!

THE CALENDAR TRICK

For this trick, you need an old calendar that shows each month in a grid, like this.

			1	2	3	4
5	6	7	8	9	10	11
12	13	14	15	16	17	18
19	20	21	22	23	24	25
26	27	28	29	30	31	

The trick

Ask a friend to draw around any 9 numbers in a block, as shown (without you peeking):

Then ask them to add up all nine numbers and tell you the answer. Say you can tell them which number is in the middle. Using a calculator, just divide the number by 9. There's your answer!

			1	2	3	4
5	6	7	8	9	10	11
12	13	14	15	16	17	18
19	20	21	22	23	24	25
26	27	28	29	30	31	

What's going on?

In any block of 9 calendar numbers, the middle one will always be the average of all the numbers—because all the other numbers are equal distances above and below it. Try it and see!

POP-UP POLYHEDRON

Make this magically appearing shape for a perfect polyhedron party trick!

A polyhedron is a 3D shape with flat sides made up of polygons. Polygons are shapes with straight sides. This polyhedron, called a dodecahedron, has 10 sides, and each side is a perfect pentagon.

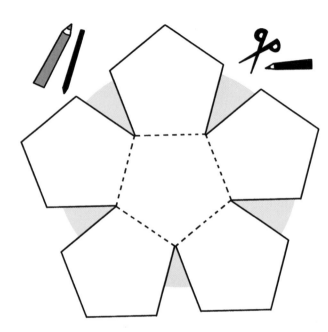

the trick

To make the polyhedron, you need an old cereal box, a ruler, a pencil, scissors, and a rubber band.

First, draw or trace two copies of this shape onto the inside of the cereal box. It's a pentagon surrounded by five other pentagons, all the same size.

Cut out the shapes, and fold along all the dashed lines in both directions, so that they bend easily.

Put one shape on top of the other, so that they overlap like this:

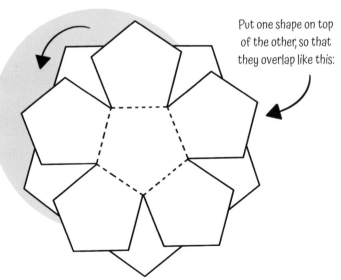

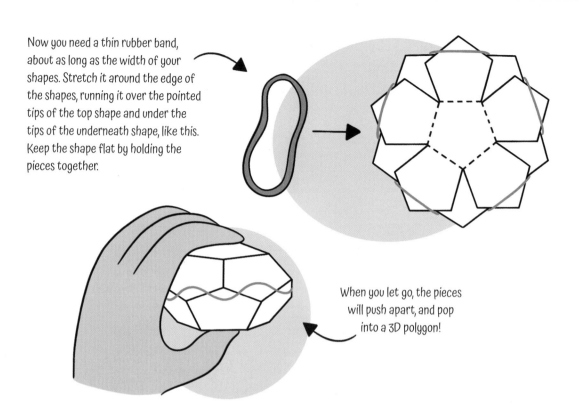

Now you need a thin rubber band, about as long as the width of your shapes. Stretch it around the edge of the shapes, running it over the pointed tips of the top shape and under the tips of the underneath shape, like this. Keep the shape flat by holding the pieces together.

When you let go, the pieces will push apart, and pop into a 3D polygon!

What's going on?

The flat pentagon flower shapes are called "nets". When the pentagons fold together, each flower forms half of the dodecahedron. When you stretch the rubber band around the tips, it pulls them inward, making the pentagons fold together, forming the 3D shape!

Why not try?

There are many other kinds of **polyhedrons.** Can you work out how to draw flat nets for making these examples?

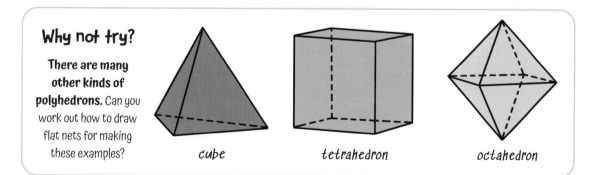

cube   tetrahedron   octahedron

HEXAFLEXAGON

This trick may be confusing at first, but once you've made your hexaflexagon, you'll love it! It's a folded paper hexagon that can endlessly turn itself inside out.

The trick

Thick or heavy paper is the best type to use.
Use a ruler, and pencil, to mark a strip along the edge of your paper, about 3 cm (1.2 inches) wide. Cut along it, then copy or trace the template below, marking it with equilateral (equal-sided) triangles.

The triangles have to be equilateral, as they must fold over each other and fit on top of each other in all directions.

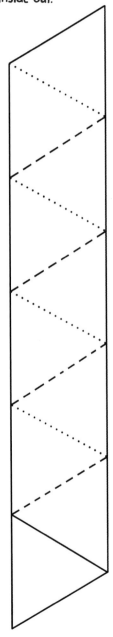

All sides are the same length.

All corners have the same angle: 60°.

60°

60°   60°

equilateral triangle

Trim any spare ends from your strip. Now fold up the strip, with the fold downward on the dotted lines, and upward on the lines with dashes and dots.

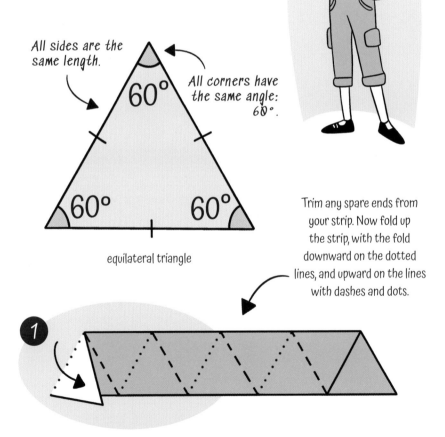

1

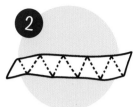

Now open out the strip.

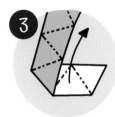

Start from one end and fold along the third fold, then the third fold after that.

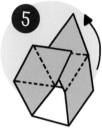

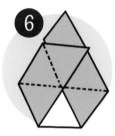

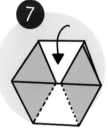

This will make a hexagon shape with one triangle sticking out.

Tuck that triangle under the first triangle.

Then fold it over and glue it to the first triangle.

To "flex" your hexaflexagon, hold it flat and fold it into three triangles, as shown. Squeeze them together, and then pull the three points out of the middle. Your hexaflexagon has turned inside out! You can do this again and again.

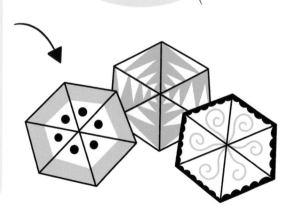

What's going on?

The way a hexaflexagon is folded means that each triangle of the hexagon is made of two layers, joined on only one side. When you flex it, they can change position, and make a new hexagon.

You can decorate each flat surface of your hexaflexagon, so that each time you flex it, a new design appears.

ROLLING UPHILL

Tell your friends or family that you can make a shape so mathematically magical, it will roll uphill! They won't believe you—but you can. However, make sure you set it all up, and try it out first, as it can be tricky to get right.

The trick

To make the magical shape, you need two cone-shaped objects.
Two straight-sided funnels work well, if they are the same size and shape. Or you can use cone-shaped wooden building blocks, if you have them, or cone-shaped packaging such as snack cones.

snack cones

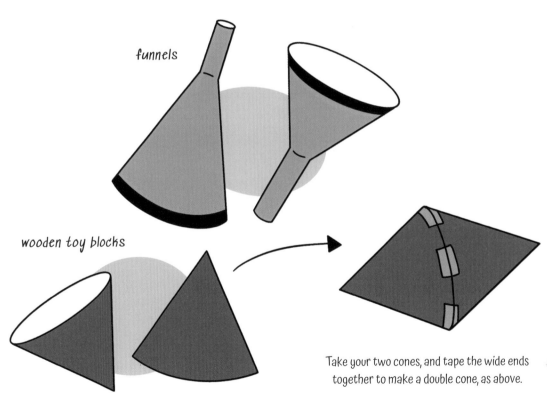

funnels

wooden toy blocks

Take your two cones, and tape the wide ends together to make a double cone, as above.

Now you need two 30 cm (12 inch) rulers, or similar long, straight pieces of wood, and some books.

Make two small piles of books, one slightly higher than the other, about 25 cm (10 inches) apart.

Place the rulers on the books in a V shape, with the point of the V at the lower end.

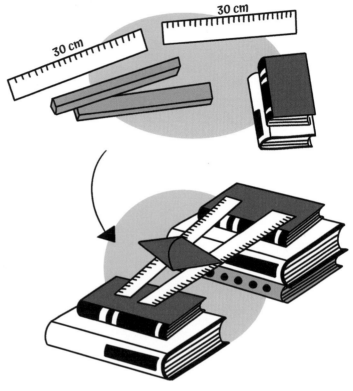

When you put your cone shape on the lower end of the V like this, it should gently roll toward the top end! Remember though, it might not work at first—you may need to adjust the slope and shape of the V until it does.

What's going on?

The reason this works is because of the sloping cone shape. At the narrow end of the V, the double cone is resting on its thickest part, near the middle. But where the rulers are farthest apart, the cone is resting on its pointed tips.

This means that the cone actually moves downward slightly on its journey—and that's why it rolls that way!

MAGIC NUMBER CARDS

This amazing magic card trick is very easy to prepare, and very hard to figure out!

the trick

First, make your own set of magic cards.
Cut out five pieces of card (cardstock), about the same size, and shape, as playing cards.

Draw lines on each card to make a grid of 15 boxes.

3 boxes across

5 boxes high

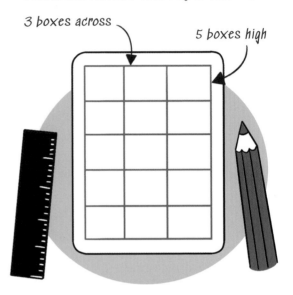

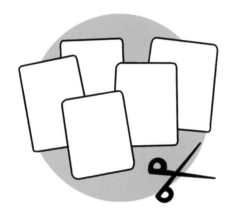

Now fill in the boxes with the numbers shown below. (You'll need to copy them exactly for the trick to work!)

Now to perform your trick! Ask your friend or family member to think of a number from 1 to 30.

Show them the first card, and ask, "Is your number on this card?" They'll answer "yes", or "no."

Do the same with the other four cards.

Whenever they say "yes" remember the first number on the card you're showing them.

In your head, add up the numbers. The result is the number they chose. Amaze them by "guessing" it correctly!

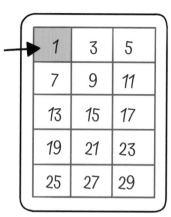

1	3	5
7	9	11
13	15	17
19	21	23
25	27	29

1	3	5
7	9	11
13	15	17
19	21	23
25	27	29

4	5	6
7	12	13
14	15	20
21	22	23
28	29	30

16	17	18
19	20	21
22	23	24
25	26	27
28	29	30

For example, if their number is 21, they'll say "yes" to these cards.

Add up 1, 4, and 16, and you get . . . 21!

What's going on?

What's the secret? It's easy when you know how!

Each number between 1 and 30 can be made using these numbers.

1   2   4   8   16

And these are the numbers that the cards start with.

For example, to make the number 21, you need one 16, one 4, and one 1.

So the number 21 appears on the cards that start with a 1, a 4, and a 16.

The same goes for all the numbers. So you can figure out any number from the cards it appears on.

Why not try?

This trick can work for bigger numbers, too. Can you figure out how to make cards that would work up to 50 or 100?

THE 17 CAMELS

This is the curious tale of the 17 camels. Can you tell how it works?

the trick

Long ago, there was an old man who had three sons. Before he died, he told his sons he would leave his herd of camels to them. The oldest son was to have half the camels, the middle son $\frac{1}{3}$ of the camels, and the youngest son $\frac{1}{9}$ of the camels.

After their father died, the sons went to divide up the camels. But there were 17 camels, and however hard they tried, they couldn't share them out as their father had instructed. Luckily, there lived a wise old woman nearby, so the three sons went to ask her advice.

"17 camels, hmm?" the old woman pondered. "I know what to do." She rode her own camel to the old man's house, and added it to the herd. "Now, try again," she said. The sons found they could divide the camels up easily.

The oldest son got half the camels—

Half of 18 = 9 camels.

The middle son got 1/3 of the camels—

$\frac{1}{3}$ of 18 = 6 camels.

The youngest son got 1/9 of the camels—

$\frac{1}{9}$ of 18 = 2 camels.

That added up to 17 camels, so the old women rode her camel home again!

What's going on?

The sons had a problem because 17 is a prime number. It can only be divided by itself, and 1—not 2, 3, or 9. By adding a camel, the old women made a herd of 18 camels—and 18 can be divided by 2, 3, and 9. The sons took $\frac{1}{2}$, $\frac{1}{3}$, and $\frac{1}{9}$ of 18, not 17. But this added up to 17, so she got her camel back!

PECULIAR PI

Pi is a number—but not a normal number, like 2, 5, or 73. Pi is what you get when you divide the circumference of a circle (the distance around the edge) by its diameter, or width.

PI OF THE PIES

Ada, Albert, and Alan have each made a pie. They want to calculate Pi using their pies.

Ada's pie:
circumference: 53.5 cm (21.1 inches)
diameter: 17 cm (6.7 inches)

Alan's pie:
circumference: 201 cm (79 inches)
diameter: 64 cm (25.1 inches)

Albert's pie
circumference: 22 cm (8.8 inches)
diameter: 7 cm (2.8 inches)

The trick

With a calculator, divide the circumference by the diameter for each pie. Do you notice anything about the results? They're all pretty much the same, because Pi is always the same!

3.1459262

What's going on?

No matter how big a circle is, its circumference is always just over 3.14 times its diameter. In mathematics, this is called a constant.

When measured very accurately, Pi is a decimal number that goes on forever.

Mathematicians have calculated Pi to trillions of decimal places using computers. To save space, they write Pi using this symbol:

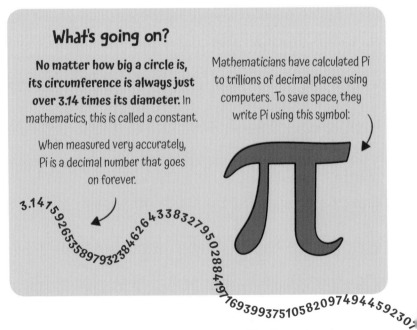

3.141592653589793238462643383279502884197169399375105820974944592307

PI TRICK

For most calculations, mathematicians round down Pi, and just use the first few decimal places: ➤ **3.141592**

the trick

Here's a handy trick to remember the first 6 places of Pi! Just memorize the phrase
"How I wish I could calculate Pi." The number of letters in each word makes Pi:

How	I	wish	I	could	calculate	Pi
3	**1**	**4**	**1**	**5**	**9**	**2**

PI POEMS

You can use the technique above to remember Pi to any number of digits.

Make up a silly sentence where each word corresponds to the correct number of letters.

Here's an example:

May I have a
3 . 1   4   1

large container
5   9

of coffee,
2   6

cream, and
5   3

sugar?
5

PI TILES

the trick

A straightened-up Pi symbol can tessellate.
That means tiles of this shape can fit together to cover a surface with no gaps. Can you figure out how?

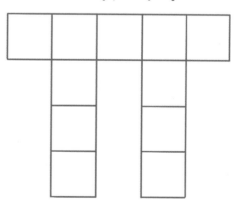

Here's the answer! ➤

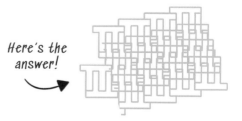

HAILSTONE NUMBERS

Hailstones bounce up and down inside thunderclouds, before finally falling to the ground. Hailstone numbers do similar!

the trick

To make a series of hailstone numbers, start with any whole number above zero.
(That means a normal number, like 6 or 23, not a fraction, or decimal number like 6.5.)

Let's start with the number ... 6

Follow these two simple rules:

If your number is even, halve it to get the next number.

If your number is odd, multiply it by 3 and add 1 to get the next number.

... so for 6, it takes 8 steps to end up at 1. On the way, the numbers bounce up, and down, then fall to the ground, like a hailstone.

6	even	halve it	= 3
3	odd	multiply by 3, and add 1	= 10
10	even	halve it	= 5
5	odd	multiply by 3, and add 1	= 16
16	even	halve it	= 8
8	even	halve it	= 4
4	even	halve it	= 2
2	even	halve it	= 1

Whatever number you start with, you always seem to end up at 1. Some numbers bounce around for longer than others. For example, if you start with 7, you get:

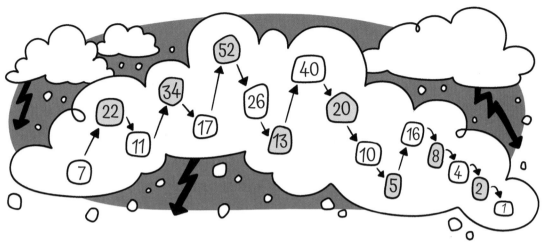

Try it with any number you like, and see what happens!

What's going on?

Nobody really knows! This trick is also known as the "Collatz conjecture," after German mathematician Lothar Collatz, who discovered it in 1937. Mathematicians have tested it with lots of numbers, and they have all ended up at 1. But we still can't be sure if it works for every single number.

Did you know?

This is the kind of puzzle that real-life genius mathematicians spend their time thinking about! They try to solve puzzles like this by finding a "proof"—a mathematical calculation that shows how the puzzle works, and whether it works for every number.

TIMES-TABLE TRICKS

Learning all your times tables can feel like a chore. Make it a little easier with these curious multiplication tricks! Multiply numbers from 1–10 by 9 easily, using just two hands.

the 9 trick

Hold out your two hands in front of you, with your fingers spread out.

Choose a number to multiply by 9, count to that finger, and bend it down. For example, for 3 x 9, bend down the 3rd finger —>

Now count the fingers to the left of the bent finger ... and the fingers to the right of it ... Put them together to make 27—and that's your answer!

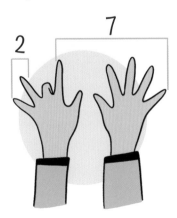

It works for all your fingers.
Here's 8 x 9:

Answer: 72!

the 11 trick

The first 10 steps of the 11 times table are quite easy, as you just double the number.

1 x 11 = 11

2 x 11 = 22

But this trick lets you multiply bigger numbers by 11 instantly. It works for any 2-digit number.

3 x 11 = 33 ... and so on.

Choose a number to multiply by 11. For example, 23.

23 X 11

Write down the 2 and the 3, with a gap in the middle.

2 _ 3

Now add together the 2 and the 3:

2 + 3 = 5

And write the result in the gap:

2 5 3 ◀

That's the answer!

Sometimes, when you add the two numbers, you'll get a 2-digit number, such as 15. If that happens, carry the 1, and add it to the first number, like this ...

78 X 11

Write 7 and 8 with a gap in the middle:	**7 _ 8**
Add 7 + 8	**7 + 8 = 15**
Write the 5 in the middle, and carry the 1	**7¹5 8**
Add the 1 to the 7	**8 5 8**

78 x 11 = 858!

FINGER CALCULATOR

Here's another finger trick that lets you multiply the 6, 7, 8, and 9 times tables using your hands.

the trick

Hold out your hands with your palms facing you, and your fingers pointing at each other, like this:

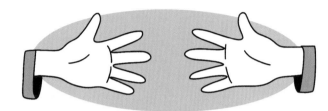

Now imagine the fingers on both hands are numbered from 6 to 10, like this:

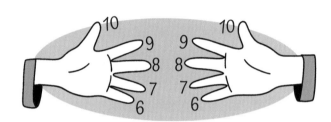

To multiply two numbers, touch the fingers for those numbers together.

So for 9 x 8, you would do this:

Now count up the two touching fingers, and all the fingers below them. This gives you the first number in your answer (the 10s).

There are 7 fingers, so the first part is 7.

7 _

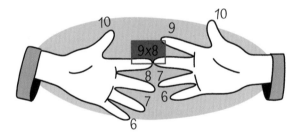

Now count the fingers above the touching fingers on each hand, and multiply them together. This gives the second part of your answer (the 1s).

There's 1 finger on the left and 2 on the right.

So that's 2 x 1 = 2

7 2

... and the answer is 72!

If multiplying the two numbers gives you a 2-digit number, carry the 1, and add it to the 10s, like this.

6 x 7

Touching fingers, plus the fingers below them = 3

3 _

Fingers above = 4 on the left, and 3 on the right . . .

4 x 3 = 12

31 2

4 2

6 x 7 = 42.

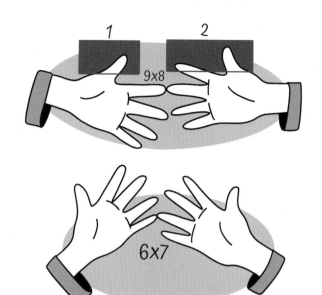

What's going on?

All these multiplication tricks basically work because we count in 10s. Numbers that are close to 10, like 9, and 11, follow patterns that are quite easy to find. The finger calculator uses 10 fingers. To find the answers, you're really just counting how far away each number is from 10. Arranging these numbers in the right order gives you the results.

Did you know?

Long ago, before computers and calculators, people used abacuses in a similar way. Different rows of beads represented 1s, 10s, 100s, and so on, and you could do calculations by moving the beads around.

SWAP THE DOTS

For this trick, the challenge is simple! Show a friend a piece of paper with two dots of different shades on it—and tell them you'll magically reverse them while the paper is folded up.

the trick

First, take a piece of paper, and draw two dots on it—for example, one orange, one black.

Make them the same size and space them out evenly in the middle of the paper.

Alternatively, you could draw two different symbols, like this:

Either way, make sure you don't use pens that will show through on the other side of the paper!

Now, put the paper in front of you, and fold it over from left to right, like this.

Then fold the back half of the folded paper over toward you, like this.

Now the paper is folded, you can pretend to do some magic by waving your hands over it, saying some magic words, or tapping with a magic wand (or just your magic finger!). To open up the paper again, start at the bottom right-hand corner.

With your left hand, pick up the corner of the top layer of paper with your finger and thumb. With your right hand, pick up the corner of the next layer underneath it.

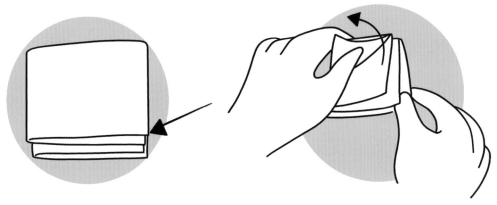

Holding these two corners, quickly open out the paper, and . . .

Ta-da! The dots have switched places!

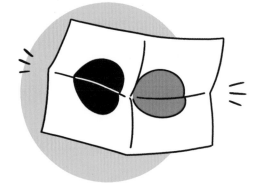

What's going on?

When you open up the paper, you're actually opening it out the opposite way from the way you folded it.
The back of the folded paper opens upward, and the whole piece of paper gets turned upside down. It's hard to spot this, because you do it quickly. And, as the dots don't have a "right way up," they just look as though they've switched places.

THE PERCENTAGE SHORTCUT

Percentages can be tricky, but they're about to get easier!

"Percent" basically means "per 100" or "out of 100." So, for example, 50% (50 percent) means one half, because 50 is half of a hundred.

A percentage problem might ask you something like: "What is 50% of 10?"

50% is a half. So 50% of 10 is 5.

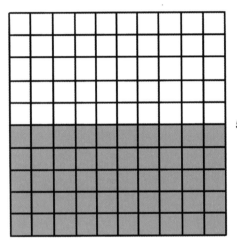

100 squares
50 squares
50 out of 100 =
50% — or half!

10 squares
5 squares
5 out of 10 =
50% — or half!

That example isn't too tricky, but some are more confusing. To make them easier, there's a clever trick you can try.

The trick

All you need to know is this amazing fact... Any percentage, such as 50% of 10, is the same the other way around! In other words, 50% of 10 is the same as 10% of 50.

Try it!

Imagine you have this problem to solve: What is 30% of 50? That's quite hard. But try swapping them around, and it might be easier. 30% of 50 is the same as 50% of 30. 50% is a half. So the answer is half of 30, which is 15.

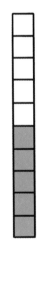

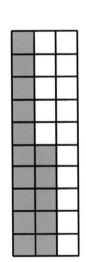

If 50% of 30 is 15...

...30% of 50 is also 15!

Here's another one ...

4% of 75? It's the same as 75% of 4.

75% is three-quarters, and three-quarters of 4 is 3.

So 4% of 75 is 3!

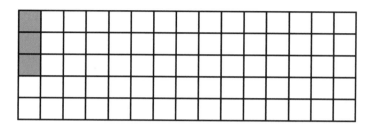

What's going on?

It may seem magical, but this trick is not as strange as it appears.
When you multiply two numbers, it doesn't matter which way around they are.

For example, 4 x 3 ...

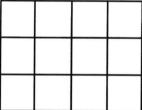

is the same as 3 x 4 ...

They are both the same thing, and both make 12.

And a percentage is really a type of multiplying.
You multiply a number by a percentage.

For example, 50% = a half.

You could also write it as 0.5

0.5 x 10 is the same as 10 x 0.5.

And 50% of 10 is the same as 10% of 50!

CURIOUS ILLUSIONS

Here are two cool optical illusions that you can use to trick your friends.
Optical illusions don't have to do only with your eyes. Some of them are also related
to numbers, and the way your brain estimates size, shape, and distance. Try them and see!

WHERE'S THE MIDDLE?

the trick

Take a look at this picture.
Which dot do you think is in the middle?

You might think it's the dot on the right,
but you'd be wrong!

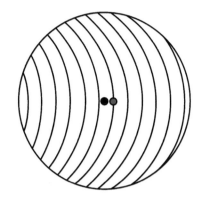

What's going on?

This illusion fools your brain's sense of space and distance. To guess where the middle of a circle is, you try to find the spot that has the same amount of space all around it.

But in the illusion, the curved lines make it look as if the space on the left side of the circle is smaller. So your brain thinks the middle must be farther to the right than it really is!

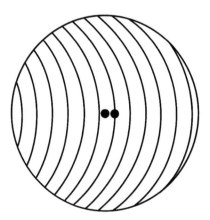

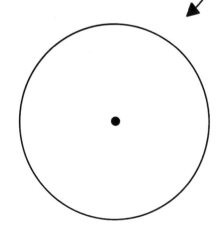

TALLER OR WIDER?

the trick

Do you think the hat is ...

a) taller than it is wide,
or
b) wider than it is tall?

In fact, its height and the width are the same! But most people see the hat as much taller than it is wide.

What's going on?

Our brains usually see vertical distances as longer than horizontal distances of the same width.
But why is that? It could be because, as humans have two eyes, most people's view of the world is a wide oval shape.

To most people, this line ...

looks longer than this line ...

... even though they're both the same.

Think about it!

You can test the theory by trying to draw a perfect square on plain paper, without a ruler.
Measure it afterward. Most people make their squares too wide, because they look taller than they are!

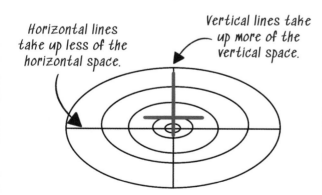

Horizontal lines take up less of the horizontal space.

Vertical lines take up more of the vertical space.

So this could make vertical lines appear longer. However, no one is really sure why.

PERFECT PERSPECTIVE

When children first start drawing, they might draw a house like this:

But an artist can draw a house that looks much more 3D and realistic, like this. They have a sense of depth and distance, known as perspective.

So how do artists make objects look 3D? Grab a pencil, and try this simple trick yourself!

The trick

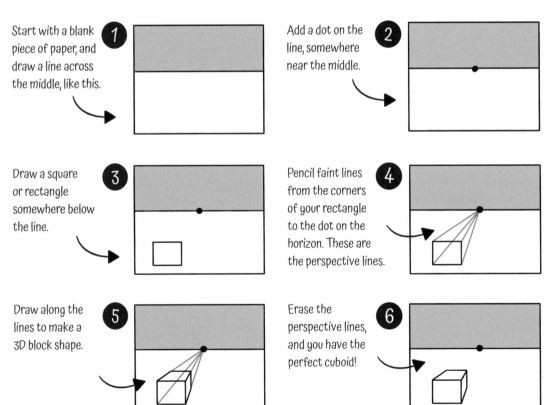

1 Start with a blank piece of paper, and draw a line across the middle, like this.

2 Add a dot on the line, somewhere near the middle.

3 Draw a square or rectangle somewhere below the line.

4 Pencil faint lines from the corners of your rectangle to the dot on the horizon. These are the perspective lines.

5 Draw along the lines to make a 3D block shape.

6 Erase the perspective lines, and you have the perfect cuboid!

You can draw as many blocks as you like in the same way, and add details to make them into buildings, furniture, or other objects.

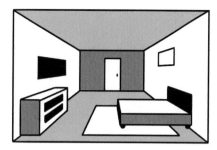

What's going on?

In the real world, we see things in 3D. As objects get farther away from us, they appear smaller. And if they are far away enough, they seem to disappear. For example, if you stand on a straight street, and look into the distance, it will appear to disappear into a single point, known as the "vanishing point."

Using a dot and perspective lines recreates this effect, and makes your picture look 3D!

vanishing point

Did you know?

You can also make a perspective picture with two vanishing points, like this. Try it!

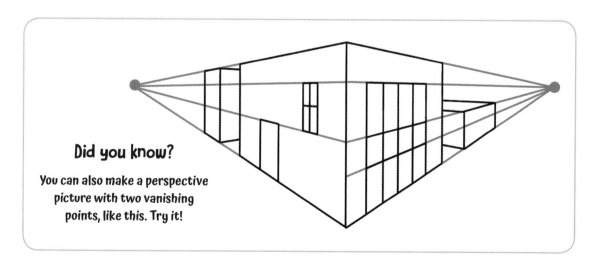

THE AVERAGE TRUTH

This curious trick is a way of guessing an unknown number. It works best if you have plenty of people to join in, such as a big family, or a school class. It's not just interesting—it could actually come in handy one day!

the trick

To try out the trick, you need lots of small objects, all about the same size, such as beads or buttons. You also need a clear jar or container to put them in.

Fill the jar or container with your beads or objects. Then ask everyone to guess how many there are. They should all write down their guesses, without telling anyone what they are (so they don't copy each other!).

Picture beads like these work well.

Now collect all the guesses, and write them down in a list, like this:

156 - Mum

345 - Dad

361 - Grandpa

555 - Granny

560 - Uncle Tariq

703 - Auntie Aisha

740 - Kemal

872 - Zaynah

1,400 - Maryam

2,828 - Hamza

Count how many guesses you have—in our list, for example, there are 10 guesses. Then, using a calculator, add up all the guesses.

Divide the answer by the number of guesses—in this case, 8,520 divided by 10.

This is your "crowd guess"—the average of everyone's guesses put together. Now for the moment of truth! Count the beads, and see how close your answer is.

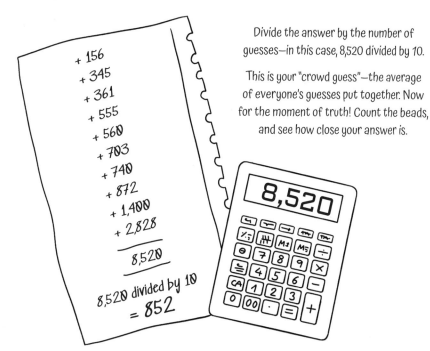

```
  + 156
  + 345
  + 361
  + 555
  + 560
  + 703
  + 740
  + 872
  + 1,400
  + 2,828
  ————
   8,520
  ————
8,520 divided by 10
     = 852
```

8,520

What's going on?

If it works, you should find your "crowd guess" is pretty good! This trick is called "the wisdom of the crowd". If lots of people guess a number, they'll mostly be wrong—but the average of their guesses will probably be close to the right answer.

Did you know?

Genius mathematician Francis Galton discovered this trick in 1906, at an English country fair, where there was a contest to guess the weight of an ox.

PERFECT PENTAGON

A pentagon is a shape with five straight sides. In a regular or perfect pentagon, the five sides are all the same length, and the corners all have the same angle.

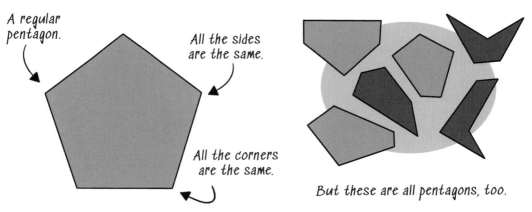

A regular pentagon.

All the sides are the same.

All the corners are the same.

But these are all pentagons, too.

Pentagons are tricky shapes. Squares, triangles, and hexagons are familiar and easy to draw, but pentagons are a lot harder.

So, if you challenge someone to fold a piece of paper into a perfect pentagon like the one above, they'll find it pretty much impossible! Try it yourself, too. How did it go?

The trick

Fear not! If you ever need a perfect pentagon in a pinch, there's actually a quick, easy, and brilliant trick that will do it in seconds!

First, measure, and cut a straight, neat strip from the edge of a piece of paper. It can be any width, but about 3 or 4 cm (1.2 to 1.6 inches) wide is easiest to start with.

Next, carefully tie a knot in the paper strip. Make sure you keep the paper flat, and pull the ends through as far as they will go. Next, flatten the knot, and fold the edges. Finally, trim off the ends, and you have a perfect pentagon!

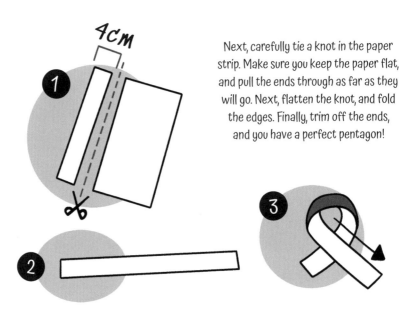

4 CM

1

2

3

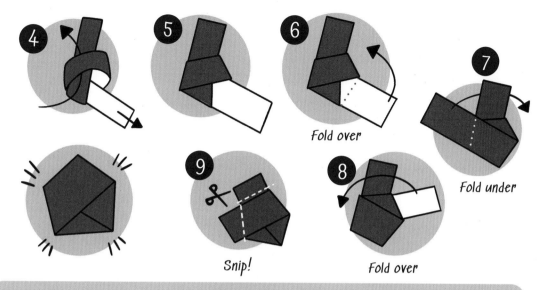

Fold over

Fold under

Snip!

Fold over

What's going on?

This works because to make a knot, the paper has to fold over itself at an angle of 108°— the same angle that's found in the corners of a perfect pentagon.

Now you can make as many pentagons as you like, large and small!

Did you know?

It IS actually possible to fold up a square piece of paper in a special way to make a perfect pentagon. But it's difficult, and it takes ages, so you'd need to be a bit of an origami expert to do it.

PARTY HATS

This hat trick seems simple, but it makes you think! You can puzzle over it on the page,
or try it on your friends. (If you have the right hats!)

the trick

**Professor Hattie Hexagon is having a birthday party.
She decides to play a game with her guests.**

She tells her friends, Maryam and Terry, to sit facing each other,
and shows them that she has three party hats—two red and one black.

Then she tells them to close their eyes, and puts the two red hats on their heads.

(She hides the black one so that they can't see it.)

When they open their eyes, Maryam and Terry can both see each other's hats, but they can't see their own hats. They have to guess which hat they are wearing, but they can't tell each other or ask any questions. First to get it right is the winner! Maryam and Terry look at each other, and think for a while. Then they suddenly both shout out, "My hat is red!" How did they know?

What's going on?

Maryam looks at Terry, and sees that he has a red hat. That means that her hat could be either red or black, because there were two red hats and one black hat to start with. But clever Maryam realizes that if she had a black hat, Terry would have shouted out immediately that he had a red hat—because there was only one black hat. That means she must have a red hat! Terry is a brainbox too, and he figures out the same thing at exactly the same time. It's a tie!

Did you know?

You can play hat games like this with three or more people, and different numbers and shades of hats. Try it, and see what happens!

THE FARMER'S SHEEP

Try this sheep-pen puzzler yourself first, then see if your friends can solve it!

The trick

Farmer Formula loves his 24 sheep. He keeps them in eight pens, arranged around his farmhouse.

The farmhouse is square with a window in each wall. As he loves numbers, too, Farmer Formula has arranged the sheep so that whichever window he looks out of, he can always see nine sheep.

For his birthday, Farmer Formula's friend, Farmer Fraction, gives him a new sheep.

"Hmm," thinks Farmer Formula. "I have to put my new sheep in one of my eight pens. But I still only want to see nine sheep from each window." How can he do this?

To help you figure out the answer, you could draw the pens on paper, like this:

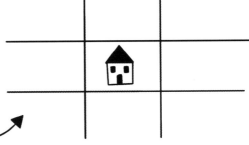

What's going on?

It can be done! But to make it work, Farmer Formula has to move some of the other sheep, too. Here's one possible answer—but there could be others.

And moved a sheep from this pen ... to this pen.

The Farmer put his new sheep in this pen.

THE FARMER'S PIGS

the trick

Meanwhile, Farmer Fraction also has an animal-penning problem.

She wants to put her nine pigs into four pigpens, so that there's an odd number of pigs in each pen.

How can she do this?

Draw the pens and pigs on paper to help you figure it out.

What's going on?

After puzzling over the problem for a while, Farmer Fraction realizes that there's a sneaky way to solve it.

She builds three pens, and puts three pigs (an odd number) in each one . . .

Then she builds a fourth pen around all of them! It contains nine pigs, so that's an odd number, too.

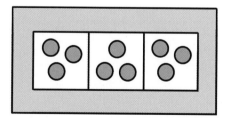

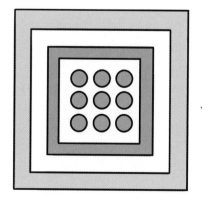

She could do it in other ways too—like this!

Can you think of any more?

CUTTING THE CAKE

Ada, Albert, and Alan are having another party! This time, they have a cake to share.

the trick

Here's the challenge to try on your friends.
They'll kick themselves when they find out how to do it!

There are 8 mathematicians at the party. They all want a piece of cake, and all the pieces of cake have to be the exact same size and shape. Easy, you might think!

You'd need four cuts to cut into slices like this:

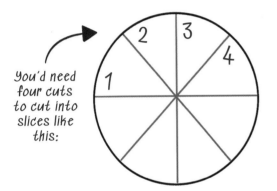

But they have set themselves a challenge . . . they must cut the cake into 8 equal pieces, but they can only cut it three times in total.

To cut eight equal slices like this, they would have to make four cuts. How can they do it with just three?

What's going on?

Did you figure it out? The answer is simple. You just need to think laterally!
Laterally means "sideways"—and that's how they have to cut the cake.

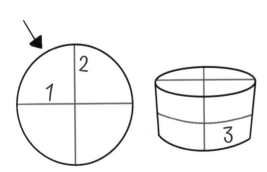

WHO WENT BALLOONING?

Here's another brain-bender that will baffle your buddies!

the trick

Millie Mathburger calls up Bill's Balloons to book a balloon ride for her family.

"There are three mothers, five daughters, one granny, three granddaughters, four sisters, and three cousins," says Millie.

"Oh, dear," says Bill. "I'm afraid there are only six spaces in the balloon."

"That's fine," says Millie. "We'll fit perfectly!"

Can you figure out how?

What's going on?

You might think it sounds as though Millie has a huge family, but think again!

Here they all are . . .

Each person has multiple roles in the family—so there are only six of them altogether!

granny
mother
daughter — sister — daughter
mother   mother
daughter — sister — daughter   daughter
cousins

HEADS AND TAILS TRICK

Amaze your audience with this mindboggling trick!
First, ask someone to blindfold you, and put three coins in front of you.

Now ask them to flip the coins to make a row of heads and tails. It can be any pattern they like, as long as it's not all heads, or all tails. For example, they might arrange the coins like this:

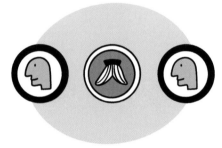

Now tell them that in no more than three moves, you will turn the coins all the same way up—even though you can't see them! To prove you're not cheating by feeling the coins, tell them to flip the coins for you.

The trick

Here's how to do it. Clutch your head, as though you're thinking hard. Then tell them to flip over the first coin in the row.

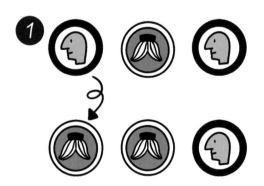

If the coins are now all the same, they'll be amazed! But if not, say: "There is still work to do!" Concentrate on the coins, then ask them to flip over the second coin.

If the coins are now all the same, take a bow! But if not, say, "This is a tricky challenge. I will have to use my third, and final move!" Act as though you're summoning all your brain power for a big decision. Then, ask them to flip the first coin again.

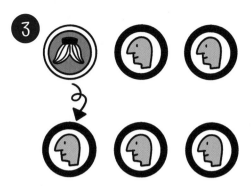

What's going on?

This cool trick works because there are only six possible patterns for the coins, and your strategy will work for all of them.

If it's one of these two patterns, then flipping the first coin works.

If it's one of these two patterns, then flipping the first coin and the second coin will do it.

And if it's one of these two patterns, you need to flip the first coin, then the second coin, then the first coin!

Ta-da!

ODD ONE OUT

This crafty coin trick will confound all your friends. You don't need any actual coins—just the power of your mind! Here's the challenge:

You have nine gold coins—or at least, that's how it looks.

However, one of them is a fake, and weighs slightly less than the others.

You can't spot the odd one out by how the coins look or feel. You can only tell by weighing them with a set of old-fashioned scales, like this:

However, you can only use the scales twice in total. How do you find out which is the fake coin?

The scales are perfectly balanced.

You put coins on the trays on either side. If one side is heavier, it will sink down.

The trick

Obviously, you could weigh every coin against every other coin, but that would probably take a lot more than two tries.
Luckily, there is a solution . . .

Divide the nine coins into three piles.

Put aside one pile, and place the other two piles on the scales.

If one coin is lighter, it's the fake.

If they're both the same, the other coin is the fake!

If one pile is lighter, that pile contains the fake. If they're both the same, the other pile (the one you didn't weigh) contains the fake. Now take the pile that contains the fake and simply repeat the process! Put aside one coin, and place the other two on the scales.

Simple!

What's going on?

As long as you can divide your coins into three equal groups, you can use this method to find the lightest group. So if you have three coins, you only need to use the scales once. If you have nine coins, you need to use them twice.

What if you could use the scales three times? You could find the fake out of 27 coins!

Spot the fake!

DRAW THROUGH THE DOTS

Here's a simple line drawing challenge that's designed to deceive your friends!

The trick

First, draw a grid of nine dots, like this:

Your challenge is to draw four straight lines, without lifting the pencil from the paper, so that the lines go through ALL the dots. (You can't fold the paper over, either!)

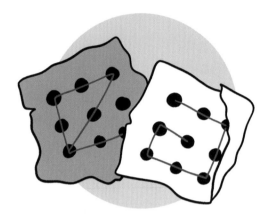

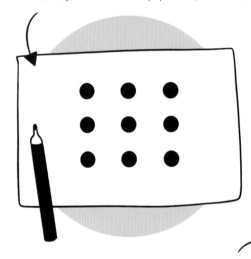

People often think they can't do it with fewer than 5 lines. But you can . . .

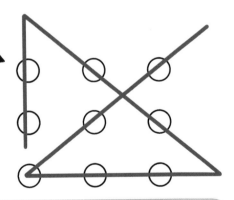

What's going on?

You need to think outside the box! To make it work, you just have to make your lines longer, so they go beyond the edges of the grid. Here's one solution . . .

Did you know?

If you're really clever, you can do it with just THREE lines. (It helps if your dots are nice and big!)

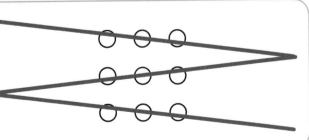

OUT OF THE WELL

A mouse has fallen down a deep well, with slimy, slippery sides.
Luckily, the mouse is unhurt, and the well is empty. But she needs to get out!

the trick

Every minute, the mouse can crawl 30 mousesteps up the wall. But then she has to stop and rest for another minute, and slips back down 20 mousesteps.

How many minutes does it take the mouse to get out of the well? See if you or your friends can get it right!

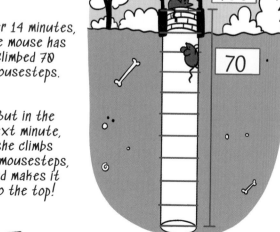

The well is 100 mouse-steps deep.

Did you think it would take the mouse 20 minutes?

Or did you get the right answer?

What's going on?

Every two minutes, the mouse climbs 30 mousesteps, and falls down 20 mousesteps.

So you might think she climbs 10 mousesteps every two minutes …and takes 20 minutes to climb 100 mousesteps. But remember, once she reaches the top, she doesn't need to stop and rest.

Total time needed: 15 minutes.

After 14 minutes, the mouse has climbed 70 mousesteps.

But in the next minute, she climbs 30 mousesteps, and makes it to the top!

100

70

THE TOUCHING COINS
FOUR-COIN CONUNDRUM

This trick sounds incredibly simple. When you challenge your friends or family to do it, they'll probably say "That's easy!" But how long will it take them to actually crack it?

The trick

You need four round coins, all of the same type, and size, and a flat table.
The challenge is to arrange the coins so that they are all touching each other. In other words, each coin has to be touching all the other coins.

But four coins don't work quite the same way.

This isn't right Each coin only touches two others, not all three.

With three coins, it's easy.

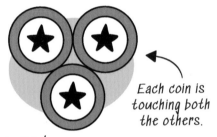

Each coin is touching both the others.

And neither's this! The coins on the left and right aren't touching.

What's going on?

So is it impossible? Of course not! Instead of laying all the coins flat on the table, put one on top of the other three—and they're all touching each other!

FIVE-COIN BRAINBENDER!

OK, maybe your friends found that easy. If so, they need a tougher challenge!

the trick

This time, you have to do the same thing, but with five coins. As with the four-coin version, you can put them on top of each other. But how?

What's going on?

Some people might just give up on this one, but there is a way.

Put one coin on the table.

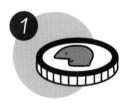

Put two more on top of it, side by side, so they touch in the middle.

EUREKA!

Stand the last two coins on their sides, on the bottom coin, but touching the other two, as well. Lean them toward each other so that they touch in the middle. Now each coin is touching all the others!

PATTERN-FILLING CHALLENGE

This challenge is one of the most famous puzzles in mathematics.
First, try it yourself, then set your friends an impossible task.

The trick

To start with, you need an outline pattern made up of lots of shapes, like this.

You can copy one of these onto paper ...

Or you could look for one on the internet, and print it out. Outline maps showing lots of countries, or counties or states, are a good option, like this map of Africa.

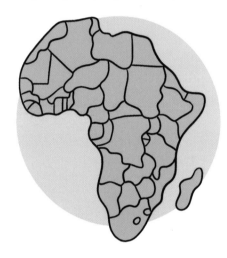

Or just draw a pattern yourself—you can use any shapes you like.

The challenge is to fill in the shapes in the pattern, using different shades of pens or markers, so that there are never two shapes of the same shade next to each other.

They can touch each other at a point, like this:

But you can't have two matching shades on both sides of a line, like this:

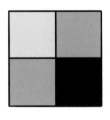
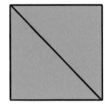

122

Most importantly of all, you have to do it using as FEW different pens as possible. What's the fewest number you can complete the challenge with?

Tip: If you don't have many markers or pens, you could use patterns instead, such as stripes, dots, and zigzags.

What's going on?

If you did it using no more than four different pens, congratulations!

Mathematicians have shown that you can fill in any pattern according to these rules with a maximum of four different shades.

Of course, some simple patterns don't need four—

But even the most complicated patterns never need MORE than four.

To challenge your friends, ask them to see if they can fill in one of the patterns with just three different pens.

Or, challenge them to draw a pattern for you to fill in that needs more than four pens. They won't be able to!

A chessboard is a good example.

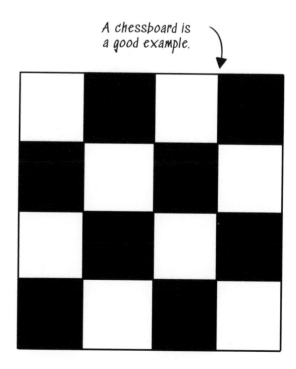

CROSSING THE RIVER

Finally, for this famous puzzle, a rabbit's life depends on you!

the trick

Mathematical genius Aisha Abacus has a tricky problem.

She needs to get herself, a fox, a rabbit, and a sack of carrots across a river, using her small boat. Why? Who knows!

The problem is, her boat is so small that she can only fit two things into it at a time—herself and one other animal or object. And she has to be in the boat, because foxes and rabbits can't row. She can cross the river as many times as she likes to get them all across. But she can't leave the fox alone with the rabbit, or the rabbit will get eaten. And she can't leave the rabbit alone with the carrots either, because the rabbit will eat the carrots.

How does she do it? And how many times does she need to cross the river? Can you figure it out?
If you can—or once you've sneaked a peek at the answer—try it on someone else!

What's going on?

The puzzle can be solved—but only if the rabbit crosses the river more than once. Here's the solution.

Aisha takes the rabbit across, leaving the carrots with the fox.

She crosses back on her own.

Now she takes the fox across.

She crosses back with the rabbit.

She takes the carrots across and leaves them with the fox again.

She crosses back on her own.

She finally takes the rabbit across.

That's seven crossings in total!

Simple!

GLOSSARY

circles into segments. There are 360° in a full circle. A right angle (the corner of a square) is an angle of 90°.

Diameter The distance across the middle of a circle.

Digit A single whole number symbol. The digits we normally use in mathematics are 1, 2, 3, 4, 5, 6, 7, 8, 9, and 0. Digits are combined to make other larger numbers.

Displace To push out of the way.

Dodecahedron A 3D shape with 12 flat surfaces—usually 12 equal regular pentagons .

Encryption The process of converting a message or other information into code.

Encryption key A number or other piece of information needed to unscramble coded information.

Engineer Someone who designs, builds, or fixes machines, engines, or structures, such as bridges.

Equilateral triangle A triangle that has all three sides of equal length.

Eureka! Ancient Greek for "I've found it!".

Exponential growth What happens when a number or amount grows faster and faster, quickly leading to a very high number.

Formula A rule or set of rules that can be applied to lead to a particular result.

Fractal A pattern that repeats itself at bigger and smaller levels of detail. However much you zoom in or out on a fractal pattern, you'll see the same pattern.

Abacus A frame with beads arranged in rows, used for doing calculations.

Anamorphic drawing A drawing that is stretched so that it looks normal when seen from a particular angle.

Average The middle or typical value of a group of numbers, found by adding the numbers together, then dividing by the number of numbers in the group.

Binary A counting system based on 2, instead of the usual base 10 (or decimal) system.

Circumference The distance around the edge of a circle.

Cog A wheel or cylinder with sticking out parts (or "teeth") around the edge, used to lock into another cog, so that one turns the other.

Constant A value or number that always stays the same, such as Pi.

Decimal number A number between two whole numbers, with part of the number written after a decimal point, such as 1.6 or 3.75.

Degrees (°) A unit used to measure angles or divide

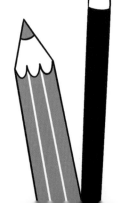

GLOSSARY

Fraction A part of a number or amount, shown as a proportion of the whole. For example, ¾ means three of four equal parts..

Gears Cogs that change the speed of rotation when one cog makes another one turn.

Hexagon A shape with six straight sides.

Hexagonal number A number of dots that can be arranged in a pattern to make a hexagon shape.

Horizontal A line or shape that runs from side to side, like the horizon.

Infinity The idea of something that is endless, and has no limit. Numbers are infinite, because there can be no biggest number.

Magic square A square of numbers in which all the horizontal, vertical and diagonal rows add up to the same number.

Magic star A star shape made up of numbers, in which all the straight lines add up to the same number.

Magic triangle A triangle shape made up of numbers, in which all the straight lines add up to the same number.

Mathematician An expert in mathematics.

Möbius strip A strip of paper or another material made into a loop with a half-twist.

Net A flat pattern or shape that can be cut out, and folded up to make a 3D shape.

Octahedron A 3D shape with eight flat surfaces.

Optical illusion A picture that confuses or tricks the brain to see something different from reality.

Pair of Compasses An instrument with a point, and a pencil holder, used for drawing circles.

Pentagon A shape with five straight sides.

Percentage A fraction or part of a whole, shown as a proportion of 100. For example, 25 percent means a quarter, as it is a quarter of 100.

Perspective The way the world looks from a particular angle, with farther-away objects appearing smaller.

Pi A decimal number, roughly 3.141592, which is the result of dividing the circumference of any circle by its diameter.

Polygon A shape with straight sides, such as a triangle, square, or hexagon.

Polyhedron A 3D shape with flat surfaces, straight edges, and pointed corners.

Prime number A number that can only be divided by itself and 1, such as 17.

GLOSSARY

Proof A demonstration that shows that an idea or theory in mathematics is true.

Radius The distance from the middle to the edge of a circle.

Regular In a regular shape, all the sides or surfaces, and the angles between them, are the same.

Right angle An angle of 90°, such as the corner of a square.

Rotational symmetry A shape that still looks the same after it has rotated into a different position.

Semicircle A half-circle.

Sequence A series of numbers that follow a rule predicting what the next number will be.

Square number A number that is another number multiplied by itself, such as 9 (which is 3 x 3). A square number of dots can be arranged in a square pattern.

Symmetrical A symmetrical shape is the same on both sides—one side is a mirror image of the other.

Tessellate A shape that can tessellate is one that tiles or fits together endlessly.

Tetrahedron A 3D shape with four flat triangular surfaces.

Triangular number A number of dots that can be arranged in a pattern to make a triangle shape.

Vertical A line or shape that runs up and down, like a lamppost.

Volume The amount of space that an object takes up.

Whole number A complete number such as 3, 10, or 200, rather than a fraction, or decimal number, such as 3 ½ or 3.5.